THANKSGIVING EVERY DAY

Discover the Blessings of Attitude with
Gratitude to God in Every Step of Your Life

ELY ROQUE SAGANSAY

Ely Roque Sagansay is the author of
Mi Daily Devotion and Christmas Every Day

WESTBOW
PRESS
A DIVISION OF THOMAS NELSON

WestBow Press books may be ordered through booksellers or by contacting:

WestBow Press
A Division of Thomas Nelson
1663 Liberty Drive
Bloomington, IN 47403
www.westbowpress.com
1-(866) 928-1240

ISBN: 978-1-4908-0635-8 (sc)
ISBN: 978-1-4908-0636-5 (e)

Library of Congress Control Number: 2013915349

Printed in the United States of America.

WestBow Press rev. date: 8/26/2013

TABLE OF CONTENTS

FOREWORD

One of the lost values that we badly needed today is Thanksgiving. In this world of materialism, people tend to forget to thank the Lord who is the source of every blessing that comes their way, whether big or small.

Pastor Ely's latest book, *"Thanksgiving Every Day"* tackles one of the common problems that besieged mankind-*ungratefulness*! This is the naked truth implicitly posed by the great Apostle Paul when he said; "Because that when they knew God, they glorified Him not as God, neither were thankful..." (Romans 1:21) I have had the privileged of being with pastor Ely when I was his assistant pastor in Asiel Baptist Church in Makati, Metro Manila. He had gone through many unfavorable and seemingly insurmountable circumstances, but he entrusted everything into the hands of the Almighty God; knowing well that eventually everything would turn out to be for His best interest and honor. He put into practice, and has been living in what is written in this book. It is therefore my strong desire that those who would read this precious book will be bless as it personally blessed me.

Reverend Eladio Datuin
Married to Enrita Guy-ab

Bachelor of Theology (BTh) International
Baptist Theological College:
Mandaluyong, Metro Manila, Philippines

Pastor- Asiel Baptist Church
Makati, Metro Manila, Philippines

Professor- International Baptist College and Seminary
Mandaluyong, Metro Manila, Philippines

DEDICATION AND SPECIAL THANKS...

Let me dedicate this book to our Lord and Savior Jesus Christ who gave me the grace to write for His honor, and the glory belongs to Him. To my wife Vem and to my children who let me work undisturbed- thank you so much. My heartfelt appreciation to all my friends, and love ones who believe in my vision and dreams... making this book possible by the grace of God.

I WAS GRATEFUL TO GOD FOR THE PAIN AND SUFFERING

(Pain, trials, and sufferings stop us
from being grateful to God)

I was in severe pain while I was typing this part of the manuscript. In a beautiful Sunday morning with so much to be thankful to God and a song in my heart; I can feel God was working in my life… and something happened. It was when I walked down to the kitchen to boil some hot water for my oat meal, and at the same time I was singing Mr. Squire Parson's song; "I Stand Amazed". The song was about what Jesus has done on the cross of which we should be thankful for… It says; "I stand amazed, I stand amazed, Of the love that hath sought me, saved me and bought me, I stand amazed…" I was enjoying the song while I was picking up the hot pot from its handle with a wet paper towel. Unfortunately, the heat of the handle gets into my thumb and burned my skin. I tried not to drop the pot, and I kept holding on unto it so I could put the pot in the sink, but to no avail. It was until I can't stand the heat of the pot, and I didn't even know that I burned my thumb real bad already. But I thank the Lord for it because it reminded me of the love of God, the salvation that I have in Christ, and the beautiful and evangelistic message of the song of my favorite singer. It also reminded me of those who died in the marathon bombing in Boston, Massachusetts and those who died in the fertilizer plant explosion in Dallas, Texas. What will happen to those who died in the explosions if they don't have the Lord Jesus Christ in their hearts? I remember the pain of those who lost their love ones to the tragedies. I can feel the pain of those who were wounded, and those who were either slightly burned or burned to first or third degree. I will never understand their pain and their suffering. For them not to be thankful is a question that only those who went through much could honestly answer. And to be thankful to God in spite of what they went through is also something only those who have a heart such as that will be commended and rewarded.

What would it feel to have a sick family member the day before Thanksgiving Day or during Thanksgiving week? Could a sick family member affect your perspective in a celebration such as Christmas or Thanksgiving Day? It's not a good question but it's indeed a reality to many homes and families. It reminds me of the movie I watched about Thanksgiving Day. This beautiful movie- "Old Fashioned Thanksgiving" was about a family who was struggling financially. All the children wanted for Thanksgiving Day was turkey, cranberry, and other good food. They especially desired to see the immediate healing of their sick mother. You can be happy or be sad on Thanksgiving Day; but remember, it's always right to be thankful. Your life, your home, and your family may be simple to others, and you may be living in a slum area; but if you are rich in love and peace- life is good for you, and it's absolutely the goodness of God working in you.

Back to my Sunday morning bad experienced in the kitchen. I was in pain for a moment with just my thumb and it was just for a while. But how about those who have died without hope and without God? My Sunday morning painful kitchen experienced was nothing compared to what others are going through, and to what Christ did on the cross for our sins. I'm not thankful for those who suffered or I could not be thankful because people are in hell or will go hell, but I'm thankful because Jesus gave us hope and salvation in Him. And I'm thankful because we don't have to go through this kind of pain. I'm thankful because someday; when it's my time to go, I will not suffer in hell for eternity. God can do the same to you if you will ask Him to come into your heart, and humbly come to Him in repentance and forgiveness of your sins. You have to believe in Him as your Savior and Lord. You must believe in His death, burial, and resurrection. If you will accept Him today; He will give you His grace, He will give you hope, and He will give you eternal life in heaven. (Romans 6:10; 23; 6: 23; John 3:16; 1: 12).

THE BRIEF HISTORY OF
THANKSGIVING

According to Wikipedia; "On December 04, 1619, 38 English settlers arrived at Berkeley Hundred, which comprised about 8,000 acres (3,200 ha) on the north bank of the James River, near Herring Creek, in an area then known as Charles Cittie, about 20 miles (32 km) upstream from Jamestown, where the first permanent settlement of the Colony of Virginia had been established on May 14, 1607.

The group's charter required that the day of arrival be observed yearly as a "day of thanksgiving" to God. On that first day, Captain John Woodlief held the service of thanksgiving. As quoted from the section of the Charter of Berkeley Hundred specifying the thanksgiving service: "We ordaine that the day of our ships arrival at the place assigned for plantacon in the land of Virginia shall be yearly and perpetually kept holy as a day of thanksgiving to Almighty God."[9]" (www.wikipedia.org)

It was during the times of the most revered, and respected president of the United States of America- president Abraham Lincoln when "Thanksgiving Day" was declared as an annual tradition and celebration in 1863. In spite of the civil war, and the conflicts between the north and the south, the racial discrimination, and the war against poverty

1

as well as the power struggle; Mr. Lincoln declared and proclaimed a national day of "Thanksgiving and Praise to Our Beneficent Father Who Dwelleth in the Heavens".

I wonder what would be in the minds of millions of people who are celebrating "Thanksgiving Day" every last Thursday of November. I have been thinking of their mind set as in term of celebrating it with a right perspective and purpose. What in President Abraham Lincoln's mind when he first proclaimed the last Thursday of November as the national "Thanksgiving Day" could be different from the people's mind set during these times. And what could be in the minds of other presidents after him? Some may celebrate it for the sake of American culture and tradition. Others may celebrate Thanksgiving Day or may just to go with the flow, but some could be serious of the occasion with praise and thanksgiving in their hearts. Thanksgiving is not just a presidential declaration or proclamation, it's something that must be received and observed with joy, with a serious and positive mind set about the occasion. We will answer those questions as we learn more about Thanksgiving Day as we explore from home and abroad.

ACCORDING TO THE BIBLE HISTORY

Is there a specific story in the Bible that could make us conclude that Thanksgiving Day has a Biblical origin? Is there a verse or a chapter in the Scriptures that we may claim as the origin of Thanksgiving Day in the Bible? We were told to be thankful by the Lord, by Apostle Paul, and in the whole Scriptures; but to claim of a specific event in the Bible is not clear enough to conclude or pinpoint such event. In Genesis 2:1- 3 it says; "1- Thus the heavens and the earth were finished, and all the host of them. 2- And on the seventh day God ended his work which he had made; and he rested on the seventh day from all his work which he had made. 3- And God blessed the seventh day, and sanctified it: because that in it he had rested from all his work which God created and made." (KJV) It says on verse two that "God ended His work... He rested on the seventh day..." That's exactly what God wanted for us to do. He gave us six days to work, and do whatever we need to do to help our family, and to fill our daily needs; but God wanted for us to rest on the seventh day. It's the time God intended for us to be at rest with Him in worship and thanksgiving. Prayer and worship must come with thanksgiving to God. Our focus must be on "giving of thanks to God" for what He has done, and what He will be doing in our lives during our fellowship together with Him. The Bible said; "24- And let us consider one another to provoke unto love and to good works: 25- Not forsaking

3

the assembling of ourselves together, as the manner of some is; but exhorting one another: and so much the more, as ye see the day approaching." (Hebrews 10:24, 25 KJV)

"Leviticus" as many Christians may say is one of the books in the Pentateuch that is hard to understand, too complicated to exercise, and irrelevant to put into practice. Its doctrine and teachings seems to be designed for highly intellectual. But, Leviticus chapter seven verses eleven to fifteen; here we read God instructed Moses regarding the Peace Offering, Thanksgiving Offering, Sacrificial Offering, and other offerings the children of Israel might present to the Lord during those times. It was simple, short and sound doctrine that even an ordinary believer during Moses' times and in our time could fully comprehend or understand. We may miss the point, and the blessing the book of Leviticus can offer to those who really dig in into His Word. God made His point and purpose through His servant Moses. The point herein was for us to offer whatever we have with thanksgiving in our hearts. In every offering, thanksgiving must be the channel to the throne of God. Apostle Paul wrote; "Continue in prayer, and watch in the same with thanksgiving;" If you offer your time to God in prayer or in the throne of His grace; be sure to come with an open hearts and with thanksgiving in your heart. In Philippians 4:6 it says; "Be careful for nothing; but in everything by prayer and supplication with thanksgiving let your requests be made known unto God." In the Old Testament, they came to God with their sacrificial and thanksgiving offerings by sacrificing animals, material or physical offerings, but in the New Testament; we have Jesus as the sacrifice once and for all. After the resurrection and the ascension of the Lord Jesus Christ- we (the Church) must come to the throne of His grace and offer ourselves as a living sacrifice. As an act of appreciation to what He has done for us; we may come to God in prayer with thanksgiving in our hearts. King David offered precious stones, Moses offered praise and songs of deliverance, the Israelites offered animals, some churches offered fruits and vegetables, others offered money, while some offered their service to God; and what will you offer to Him right now?

Apostle Paul wrote; "Thanks be unto God for his unspeakable gift." (2 Corinthians 9:15 KJV) What do you think Paul would have in mind when he wrote to the Corinthian church? In verse one, Apostle Paul mentioned about their ministry to the saints or fellow believers. Personally, it's something that I am thankful to God when I'm doing something for His church or God's people. It is an honor to be of service to the King of kings and to His servants. We may not always have this kind of opportunity in the kingdom of God. But Apostle Paul also mentioned of the forwardness of their mind and their zeal. Notice verse "2- For I know the forwardness of your mind, for which I boast of you to them of Macedonia, that Achaia was ready a year ago; and your zeal hath provoked very many." (2 Corinthians 9:2 KJV) What does Paul have in mind when he said; "the forwardness of your mind..."? What is "Forwardness" anyways? In some Bible versions it means "eagerness" "readiness" or "willingness". (ESV, NIV, CEB)

These are little things with great impact in the Lord's kingdom and in the life of His saints. And being thankful to God is actually the outward and inward outcome, and spiritual manifestation of having the forwardness of mind in the kingdom's work. You don't dwell in your past or failure, and you don't live with complain and a heavy hearts. Instead, we should be thankful to God for little things that we've done, and we are doing for the Lord of which only eternity could tell of how it may have worked, and may have moved the life of those around us.

Now in verse 5, Paul was talking about the bountiful blessings that they have from the Lord. Have you ever thought of why God is blessing you with so much? Have you ever thought of why God placed the under privileged in your path? Or have you ever thought of why God opened the door of unspeakable blessings to you of which could be beyond your imagination? If you would think of the good paying job, the good health, and all the goodies that others may not even have in their whole life time… and being thankful should be your first on the list. After all the positive traits, and the things Paul said about the believers; he expounded to them the Lord's principles, especially the principle of 'sowing and reaping'. Notice the following verses; "6- But this I say, He which soweth sparingly shall reap also sparingly; and he which soweth bountifully shall reap also bountifully. 7- Every man according as he purposeth in his heart, so let him give; not grudgingly, or of necessity: for God loveth a cheerful giver. 8- And God is able to make all grace abound toward you; that ye, always having all sufficiency in all things, may abound to every good work: 9- (As it is written, He hath dispersed abroad; he hath given to the poor: his righteousness remaineth for ever. 10- Now he that ministereth seed to the sower both minister bread for your food, and multiply your seed sown, and increase the fruits of your righteousness;) 11- Being enriched in everything to all bountifulness, which causeth through us thanksgiving to God. 12- For the administration of this service not only supplieth the want of the saints, but is abundant also by many thanksgivings unto God; 13- Whiles by the experiment of this ministration they glorify God for your professed subjection unto the gospel of Christ, and for your liberal distribution unto them, and unto all men; 14- And by their prayer for you, which long after you for the exceeding grace of God in you. 15-Thanks be unto God for his unspeakable gift." (2 Corinthians 9:6- 15 KJV)

A thankful individual is a giving individual in spite of difficulties and negative circumstances in life. If you check out or study the personality of churches, and the people that has been blessed with so much are those who give in spite of difficulties and unpleasant circumstances. What is your attitude toward God, and His people or His church in term of your service in giving? We can easily get distracted with money or blessings, and forget about the source and provider of such. And we must have the right attitude toward His church in our giving of our tithes and offering as well as our giving for the cause of missions. We may also easily get discourage by the uncontrolled circumstances around us. As Christians, one of the encouragements we have in God is His righteousness and His holiness. In God's attributes, we can surely give tribute, and be consistently grateful for Who He is in our lives. (Psalm 97:12) When David was the king of Israel; he encouraged his people to give thanks to

God. King David mentioned of the greatness and attribute of God in his prayers. He did the same thing during the time when they brought the Ark of the Covenant, and when they offered the sacrifices and the burnt offerings to God. (I Chronicles 16:1- 43) This may not be a big deal to other religious groups, but to Christians; this should be received and shared with seriousness. We may commit the sin of sacrilege unconsciously if we offer and worship God with complaint and with ungrateful hearts.

David here even appointed the Levites to minister, record, and to thank the Lord as recorded in verse four. In I Chronicles 16:7 it says; "Then on that day David delivered first this psalm to thank the Lord into the hand of Asaph and his brethren." It's a blessing to know that David's first point in his sermon, and worship songs composition was about gracefulness, thankfulness or giving of thanks to God. It's very compelling to read the following verses- Once you read verse 8, you can't stop reading the following verses of this book and chapters. The power of the Word of God and the joy of reading and meditating on David's attitude are amazing and awesome. We can see here the people's response to the Lord in worship with thanksgiving was amazing and way different from how the Christians of this present time responded in worship.

The essence of thanksgiving was on the preaching and teaching of the Lord Jesus Christ. (Luke 17:11- 19; 6:32- 33) The elements of Thanksgiving Day in the Scriptures are in the writings of Apostle Paul. (I Corinthians 14:17; Ephesians 1:16; Philippians 1:3) The idea of the celebration of "Thanksgiving

Day" was introduced by Moses after the Exodus, and the victory at the crossing of the Red sea when Moses sang praises to God. The dedication of the temple during the times of Kings Solomon and David were filled with praises and giving of thanks. Even when the Israelites had the Ark of the Covenant during King David's times- the giving of thanks was a big deal. It was recorded accurately, and in common words that even the common people during their times could easily understand it. (I Chronicles 16:7- 34 23:30; 29:13) We experience the grace of God overflowing toward us. The sufficiency that we have in Christ, and in all that God has bestowed upon us are for His purpose, and toward good works on our part. The ministry is a blessing in itself, but there is no greater blessing than to have the Lord's hands and presence in our work for Him. We should be thankful to God for the ministry that He entrusted us. And King David showed through his testimony. It's very obvious on the testimony and writings of God's people both in the Old and New Testament era. And it's still at work in our generation and will be effective for the generations to come.

The Lord's teaching has not changed, and we are expected to do the same. His way of performing miracles, and how He showed His power through His anointed prophets and followers by what they did during their times may be different from what we've experienced; but the message and His teaching is still the same. To the Corinthian and Macedonian churches; it should be about the apostles' teachings, philosophy, and principles of teachings in giving and handling of God's blessings. It is to be grateful and learn to "pay it forward". The CEO of many huge earner companies is into "Pay it Forward…" philosophy by being involved in a charitable organization. To be grateful is to be charitable in some ways. If you can't be charitable you could be miserable. A grateful heart is a giving heart. Some people are just waiting, longing and looking for charities and gifts, while others are working hard to be a part of it. Some people are used to receiving a gift or be a recipient than to be a part of sharing and giving.

A HEARTFELT GRATITUDE

The great Job of the Old Testament went through a roller coaster of pain, sufferings, trials, rejection, and criticism. In spite of what he went through, he maintained a rightful attitude and a grateful spirit with God. In his hopeless situations, he wrote; "And where is now my hope? As for my hope, who shall see it?" (Job 17:15KJV) In (NIV) it says; "15- Where then is my hope- who can see any hope in me?" It's the same question people from many parts of the world are asking. And many of them asked the same question after they were at the end of their rope, because of their beliefs and faith in false hopes.

We placed our hopes on people, on human wisdom, human strength and capabilities. We let God watch us on the sideline as we play our own game which is bound for destruction. It's not that God don't care about us, but it's because we ignore Him, and we disguised our doubt and fear in the name of self pity instead of trusting Him. What He can do to us and for us is in His hand and for His glory. And if God will do something great in our lives, we have the tendency to overlook Him and be ungrateful to Him. And because of this prevalent attitude of having an ungrateful attitude on what God has done, and have been doing in our lives; my friendly advised- start your personal journal regarding the things that you should be thankful to God for, be it personal blessings or general blessings. Notice my personal expression of my gratitude to God…

I Express My Heartfelt Gratitude to God for the Hope that I Have in Christ. The world may place their hope in things or people, but you cannot deny the truth that salvation is from God in Christ. I thank the Lord because my salvation is not based in religion, as we all know that religion and religious denominations has failed us in many ways. I praise God because my salvation is not seated or standing in the sand or in the hands of man; but my salvation, and my hope is in Christ- the solid ground. He is the only Savior of the lost world. My hope is not in man but in God. And I wish everyone will have the same hope and the same gratitude in God our Savior. The Bible says; "13- Looking for that blessed hope, and the glorious appearing of the great God and our Saviour Jesus Christ; 14- Who gave himself for us, that he might redeem us from all iniquity, and purify unto himself a peculiar people, zealous of good works." (KJV) Apostle Paul wrote; "23- And not only they, but ourselves also, which have the first fruits of the Spirit, even we ourselves groan within ourselves, waiting for the adoption, to wit, the redemption of our body. 24 For we are saved by hope: but hope that is seen is not hope: for what a man seeth, why doth he yet hope for?" (Romans 8:23- 24 KJV)

I Express My Heartfelt Gratitude to God for My Home with Christ in the Center. Joshua could be known to many as the second man of Moses, a warrior, and a faithful servant of the Lord. Joshua was also a family man. I believe he loves his family, and he has his family's support. Joshua's family faithfully served with him in his work for God. No wonder he has the authority to say these… "14- Now therefore fear the LORD, and serve him in sincerity and in truth: and put away the gods which your fathers served on the other side of the flood, and in Egypt; and serve ye the LORD. 15- And if it seem evil unto you to serve the LORD, choose you this day whom ye will serve; whether the gods which your fathers served that were on the other side of the flood, or the gods of the Amorites, in whose land ye dwell: ***but as for me and my house, we will serve the LORD.*** " (Joshua 24:14- 15 KJV)

We don't have a perfect home and I don't have a perfect family, but one thing for sure; Jesus is the head and the driver of our little house, and our Christian home. He is the King, and the wisdom of every decision we make. I thank the Lord because I know Christ is in the heart of my children, and I've watched them try to live a Christ centered life as they grow physically, emotionally, and spiritually. They serve the Lord with me in my church and ministries. I have a loving wife who love and serve our Lord in so many ways. There might not be some turkey and cranberry on the table; but you can have each other on Thanksgiving Day. We may be poor in property or material and in financial prosperity; but we are richer than a king in family. A beautiful phrase I got from a wall décor in one of the house I visited says; "My house is small. No mansion for a millionaire, but there is room for love and there is room for friends, that's all I care."- Unknown

JOSEPH THE PRIME MINISTER OF EGYPT

Joseph made it as the new prime minister of Egypt, but it did not come to him easy, and he did not get it the easy way. Joseph was marred, molded and mended on his way from the pit to become a prisoner, and he became the prime minister of Egypt. One of the stepping stones that he has to climbed was the attitude of his ungrateful brothers, the ungrateful wife of his master Potiphar, and his ungrateful best friend in prison.

The Ungrateful Friend of Joseph

We have friends and along with trusted friends are best friends. The big question could be; how long and how far can we trust our friends, best friends or trusted friends? I heard people say to their best friend a "Traitor!" "Disgusting!" and all kinds of negative adjectives! Sometimes you can't just blame them because of their hurt, and the pain their friends have caused them to suffer.

Joseph has his own unforgettable experienced when his friends did something hurtful to him. It happened after Joseph helped his friend gain his freedom, and a good paying job. (Genesis 40:1- 23) The saddest part in Joseph's life's story is in the last verse of Genesis forty. In verses 21 to 22 it says; "21- And he restored the chief butler unto his butlership again; and he gave the cup into Pharaoh's hand: 22- But he hanged the chief baker: as Joseph had interpreted to them." But notice verse 23 as the saddest part of Joseph's long and good bonding relationship as friends with the butler and a baker was unfolding to a negative ending. In verse "23-Yet did not the chief butler remember Joseph, but forgat him." (KJV) Someone could identify with what Joseph went through. There are people or friends who can easily betray our trust and friendship.

I was in a Christian family garage sale looking for some deals and good stuff to send to the Philippines for pastors and missionaries that we are supporting. The beautiful paragraph written in a nice marble and a porcelain table décor that caught my attention, and made me set up the camera on my iphone and took a picture of the notes about friendship. It says;

"Recipe for Friendship

Take two heaping cups of patience,
One heart full of love,
Two hands full of generosity
A dash of laugher,
One head full of understanding,
Sprinkle generously with kindness,
Add plenty of faith and mix well;
Spread over a period of a lifetime,
And serve everybody you meet."- Unknown

Joseph's Life and Service
(A Grateful Immigrant in Egypt)

Millions of people from all over the world come or migrate to the United States to live and stay for good. Some became successful but others failed, and became more miserable. I have the opportunity to talk to some of the immigrants here in Michigan, and I heard different outlook, attitude, and perspective in life as immigrants. Some were grateful while others were critical of the government as their way of exercising their "Free Speech". But to attack, bomb or destroy its own citizens would be a different story. It's still fresh in my mind of what happened to the Boston Marathon bombing victims. The world watched in awe live on television. The brothers who were once a refugees from Russia, and became a US citizen only to bomb and kill those who paid for their flight, their education, and freedom to the United States of America was unacceptable!

Joseph has a different way of "Paying it Forward" when he lived and served his adopted country. Joseph even served Egypt while in prison. Notice what the Bible says; "1- And it came to pass after these things, that the butler of the king of Egypt and his baker had offended their lord the king of Egypt. 2- And Pharaoh was wroth against two of his officers, against the chief of the butlers, and against the chief of the bakers. 3- And he was bound. 4- And the captain of the guard charged Joseph with them, and he served them: and they continued a season in ward." (Genesis 40:1- 4 KJV)

Joseph was once the prince of prison who served his fellow prisoners. You may have a stable position in the government, at church or in an organization which is good if you have a servant's heart. If you are serving others with sincerity of heart, and in the name of Jesus; such spirit will smoothly flow in you like a river. In (Genesis 39:21- 23) it says; "21- But the LORD was with Joseph, and showed him mercy, and gave him favour in the sight of the keeper of the prison. 22- And the keeper of the prison committed to Joseph's hand all the prisoners that were in the prison; and whatsoever they did there, he was the doer of it. 23- The keeper of the prison looked not to anything that was under his hand; because the LORD was with him, and that which he did, the LORD made it to prosper." (KJV) If you dig deeper as recorded in (Genesis 41:14), here we can read and may observe that Joseph shaved to serve, and this time he is serving the king of Egypt. In chapter forty, he served the prisoners and the prince of prison, but the scenario has changed, this time when he was called to serve the King of Egypt, but his service to King Pharaoh and the Egyptians were actually a service to the King of kings. God reduced Joseph to nothing, and made him exercised the spirit of "servant attitude" for a greater purpose. God sometimes will reduce us to nothing so we can be grateful with Him and of Him.

We can see the sincerity of Joseph when he gave his life to serve his father Jacob by serving his brothers as a delivery boy, and a watcher in behalf of his dad. The Lord took him to Mr. Potiphar's house where he became the manager of Potiphar's household. Notice what it says; "3- And his master saw that the LORD was with him, and that the

LORD made all that he did to prosper in his hand. 4- And Joseph found grace in his sight, and he served him: and he made him overseer over his house, and all that he had he put into his hand. 5- And it came to pass from the time that he had made him overseer in his house, and over all that he had, that the LORD blessed the Egyptian's house for Joseph's sake; and the blessing of the LORD was upon all that he had in the house, and in the field." (Genesis 39:3- 5 KJV) But it did not end in misery, but in prosperity and blessings.

What is it in the idea of "Paying it Forward" on Thanksgiving Day, Christmas Day or Mother's Day, and other special holidays like Veterans Day? It may mean you pay for someone else's meals in a drive thru or in a restaurant. It may mean paying for a bus fare, a train fare of a mother or a student. It means giving, and sharing of a little gift or something to the war victims, or helping the needy and injured soldiers. This is thanking God by sharing what God has given us. It means giving back to God by sharing, and giving to the poor and less fortunate.

The reward of being a servant and to be able to serve God and our fellowmen is enormous. We serve the Lord with sincerity of heart and mind. I have a friend who is now serving in the military, and actually he is stationed in one of the war zones, a very dangerous area. As we talked and enjoy our time together, I happened to asked him about his service in the military, and why he'd chosen to serve than to be out there having a good time or may be start a business. I was surprised when he said; "Pastor, it is my privilege to serve this country, our people, especially these young people, and the little children so they could have their freedom. It is my joy to see these children playing basketball because they have the freedom to do so." I have a high respect for people like my friend who unselfishly, sincerely, and lovingly served our country and our people so we can enjoy our freedom. We need these kinds of people who are willing to sacrifice, and give their lives in the name of freedom, service and love. And we owe them our gratitude.

We are the Lord's soldiers, and we are serving the Lord of Hosts, and He desires our love and sacrifices for the name of our King and Lord. The Apostle Paul has the full authority as a soldier of God to tell us to follow the Lord of Hosts. In the book of (Romans 12:1- 2), it says; "1- I beseech you therefore, brethren, by the mercies of God, that ye present your bodies a living sacrifice, holy, acceptable unto God, which is your reasonable service. 2- And be not conformed to this world: but be ye transformed by the renewing of your mind, that ye may prove what is that good, and acceptable, and perfect, will of God." (KJV) I believe that service is one of the best and worthy things a person can do to express his/her gratitude to individuals, company or country he or she is indebted. And most of all; it's the best for our Lord, King, Savior and Creator of whom we are grateful for giving us this life and the life to come.

HOW DO WE CELEBRATE
THANKSGIVING?

We Were so Thankful We Were Stuck at the Airport. On our way back to Detroit, Michigan from a mission trip to the Philippines; we were stuck in Honolulu, Airport. We were so thankful to God for letting us sleep for a night at the airport because we were expecting an early morning flight to California then straight to Detroit. It was our 26xth wedding anniversary, and it has been our dream to visit Hawaii, but it's too expensive for the 2 of us to fly and stay there for a week. But my wife and I were blessed to have our flight being delayed in Manila, then in Hawaii. By God's intervention and God's provision, He let us visit Hawaii for free. We expected to fly the next day, but there was no available flights for us due to spring break. So we decided to call our new friends Joe and Ann Hurst. I met missionaries Joe and Ann Hurst in Bulacan, Philippines during our mission trip. Pastor Arturo "JR" Raymundo, my brother in law introduced them to us. We stayed in their home for a night and a day. Pastor Joe shared to me about his life in Detroit, Michigan and his ministry in Hawaii. They ministered to the Filipino people through music and arts, because Ann is a professional artist and Joe is a good musician, and their daughter helped them in their ministry with children.

How Can Thanksgiving Day be Use for an Effective Ministry?
Joe and Ann shared to us how they used their home for
the Lord, and use it to bless others on Thanksgiving Day.
Pastor Joe shared to the Filipinos that he ministered unto in
the Philippines about thanksgiving, and how they celebrate
it in Hawaii. He invites people to come to their home for
Thanksgiving Day dinner. Remember Hawaii is a very
diverse place like California. You have Samoans, Japanese,
Filipinos, Chinese, and other cultures. They prepare variety
of foods expecting their visitors would be coming from
different cultures. They prepared imu pork, rice, lumpia,
kalua, and other local foods.

Thanksgiving in Joe's house is a big event, and something
that they really work hard, and prepared for to make it
enjoyable. They have time for praises and testimony where
they shared their blessings as they stand or sit around
the table. It would be a time to thank God for healing
relationships that has been restored, or restored marriages
and children that have come home. What makes it exciting
is the testimony of God's grace and miracle. The great
thing about it is when there are unbelievers around, and
they can make them comfortable, and not be felt threaten
by the atmosphere of the presence of God fearing people. I
asked Joe if they share the gospel to the visitors at the table.
He said; "No, it's not like we're telling them you better
turn or burn… or before you eat that turkey you need
to take my Jesus first…" They made sure the unbelievers
are comfortable, and not felt like they're trying to convert
them to Christianity. They were not trying to evangelize
everybody at the dinner table, but they get to hear the

praises, the miracles, and what God has done, and what God is doing in the life of His children.

They don't ask the unbelievers to share their stories or blessing, they just let them pass their turn. It's a blessing to know that we have brothers and sisters on the other parts of the world who used Thanksgiving Day for a good purpose, and for the glory of our God. I asked Joe if he was given the opportunity to preach on Thanksgiving Day, what would be his preaching. His response; "I would be preaching about the American tradition of celebrating Thanksgiving Day, and I will be preaching about Christ's death." He said he will put emphasis on what Christ has done for us and we must be thankful to God for sending us His Son, and for His suffering on the cross. He was spat upon. He was scourged, and nailed on the cross. He was thankful to God for what He has done for him; taking away the sins that he's committed, and was placed in Jesus on the cross. In spite of inconveniences, the trials that they went through in the Philippines during their stay there; Joe and Ann were thankful because it was all covered by God's blessings and miracles.

They Don't Have the Money. Before Joe and Ann left for the Philippines with their only daughter Aliah Ann; they didn't have the money for the trip. So they asked their friends for prayers, and for their needs. But they were convinced, and they felt what God wanted them to do and God wanted them to go. They absolutely knew that God was just waiting for them to say; "Yes Lord". But when those days came for him to say; "Yes Lord..." The very next day; Joe found

$1,700 dollars underneath their mattress. He realized he saved those a long time ago, and didn't even remember it, and obviously forget about it. The Lord performed a miracle. The money was good enough to buy the tickets. Joe took it as a sign and a confirmation from God. He said; "It was like a revelation from God. We just really have to trust and obey. The Lord will provide if we only abide in Him and in His Word."

He was Grateful for Those Who Partnered with Them. Joe said; "People and friends started calling me and committed help for our trip to the Philippines. We were provided for all of our needs right to the very last day". Joe had enough money to leave, and pay for the extension of his visa in the Philippines. He had enough money to pay for his extra luggage and other expenses. He said; "God is just right on Time with our need, and that's the way He works, and we see miraculous things". When asked what he thinks of the Filipino people during his visit to the Philippines, he said; "Filipinos are very courteous, thankful and attentive or good listeners."

I have my personal testimony regarding God's provision in our "Mission Trip 2013" in the Philippines. We don't have an alotted BUDGET for the trip because we are taking it by faith. We also see God's hand upon us in His provision. We need to trust the Lord for the work that we are doing in His field. I shared my testimony to my friends, in my preaching, and to the pastors in the Philippines during our mission trip. It was four days before we left for the trip to Manila when I asked my wife how much money she had in her bank for the trip? I got a direct, precise, and definite answer. She said; "Five dollars in my checking account and that's it." I said; "You have more money than me, then." My wife asked; "How much money did you saved for the trip?" I said; "Two dollars and forty nine cents in my checking account." But we're thankful for God's provision; we made it in the Philippines with cash in our pockets on our way back to Detroit.

a) How Apostle Paul Celebrate Thanksgiving

Apostle Paul in the book of Colossians 1:3- 5 said; "3- We give thanks to God and the Father of our Lord Jesus Christ, praying always for you, 4- Since we heard of your faith in Christ Jesus, and of the love which ye have to all the saints, 5-For the hope which is laid up for you in heaven, whereof ye heard before in the word of the truth of the gospel;" (KJV).

Paul here was thankful to God for the believers who continued in the faith, in the love of God, and hold on unto the hope that they have in the Lord Jesus Christ. It's obvious that Paul was not celebrating Thanksgiving Day when he wrote this epistle, but one thing for sure; to be thankful, and to be grateful for him was a daily habit, a daily exercise or a daily positive attitude. He wrote; "In everything give thanks: for this is the will of God in Christ Jesus concerning you." (1 Thessalonians 5:18 KJV) Obviously, for Apostle Paul- the giving of thanks was not just in every good thing, but in everything. It is not just during Thanksgiving Day but every day. It will not be on the positive things, but on the negative side of life. It must not just be on good times, but in bad times, and when you are in your deepest moment in life. A "Thank you…" must not be said, and written in response to a good deeds on your behalf or for your sake and advantage, but even if you become a recipient of the evil deeds by anyone. Why? Because at least you know you have a positive mind set. We now we're not in control, because God is in control, and we will have the opportunity to trust Him for it. We must avoid the negative tendency of being the initiator of something that's not pleasing to God and to men.

I enjoy the gentleman in our plane who served us on our flight to California. This man will always say; "Thank you for thanking me…" And those who appreciate him would give him a big smile of how or the way he said it too. You can see the joy in his facial expression as well as with those who appreciated his positive attitude. Apostle Paul has so much more of it.

b) How Do You Personally Celebrate Thanksgiving?

Did you know, and do you believe that celebrating Thanksgiving Day must not only be a national celebration for each individual, but must be a personal celebration too? How do you celebrate thanksgiving is a catchy and a good question. The question of why, how often, and what makes us celebrate the occasion is more of a personal than a general question. You can answer such question in a way that pleases you. It's disturbing for me to know that some of the people I know got drunk on Thanksgiving Day. It should be a day where families would gather together to pray, and thank the Lord for all His goodness and blessings. It should be the time where everybody at home is with a clear mind, right perspective, good conscience, and in the spirit of love, forgiveness and humility. I personally believe that everyone can use Thanksgiving Day occasion as a day for restoration, reconciliation, and repentance. It should be a day of forgiveness, and a day for all of us to forget the past, and be thankful for this life, and the life to come with the Father in heaven.

c) How Do Your Family Celebrate Thanksgiving?

A Time to Celebrate with the Family, and for God's Glory! Christmas and thanksgiving are 2 special days that we don't want to miss for lunch or dinner together as a family. I hated it when I can't be with my family during those special days. One thing for sure; the center in millions of homes in America on Thanksgiving Days are the turkeys, cranberry, drinks and a reunion of a family. And we know it because it's a tradition and it's our culture. But other than having turkey, food; some homes have wine and drinking session as part of their celebration, what else could be the happenings? Other than thanksgiving sale or black Fridays, and black Saturdays sale; what else do you have in mind and may have observed? Are you bound to observe what could be the tradition, and the common celebration of Thanksgiving Day?

It should be a special time for our love ones, and to be with our love ones. I wonder if people from the other side of the world would be willing to make Thanksgiving Day as a reunion day. Is it possible for families around the world to make both Christmas and Thanksgiving Day set aside for family reunion? It should be a huge family gathering or a whole day celebration. I love watching "Thanksgiving Day Parade" on TV with my family. I believe that that's one of the show that I am comfortable sitting with my family, and not be worried on what we would be seeing next on the screen, especially if I'm with my under age son. The reason why I mention it is to share with you what we usually do as a family on Thanksgiving Day. It doesn't have to be a movie day or a game day, but it would be great to be together under one roof or be together for lunch and dinner. This is a once a year celebration, it means the time, the day, the planning, and how you will do it must not be a problem. We have the whole year to set it, plan it, and pray for it. Make Thanksgiving Day your everyday life by being thankful for your family and for this life. If you are a parent; help, teach, and lead your family to the Lord's sanctuary of praise and thanksgiving.

We don't want to change anything that has been structured for a purpose and with a purpose, but we can do something different to touch lives, and to stick us together as a family, and keep us closer to God. I remember a co- worker who gave me a turkey on Thanksgiving Day with an encouraging words he said; "I just want to share this to you as my way of saying 'Thank you' to you, Ely..." A little thing or a small turkey shared in the name of Christ can change an individual's lives or touch the heart of the poor and needy. Have you ever thought how our world would look like if thanksgiving and other holidays would be celebrated like Christmas days where people give and share their love and gifts? I was thinking of Memorial Day or Veterans Day where Americans would join hands together to help our War Veterans or share something for the elderly or senior citizens. I met a World War II veteran in California. Mister Morris fought in the Philippines with the Filipino soldiers against the Japanese. I asked him what he wanted to hear from this generation for risking his life for the freedom of millions. He said; "Just a thank you".

My family celebrates Christmas with gift giving by helping some of the pastors and missionaries and the less fortunate in the Philippines. We sometimes send cash and we also send out boxes of clothes and toys for children. On Thanksgiving Days; we invite some of the pastors and friends to join us for lunch or dinner. Imagine if each home in every part of the world will have this kind of celebrations. I assure you, we will have a better world. Having a different perspective in life, a godly, and Christ centered way of celebrating thanksgiving can change our homes, and can change lives.

d) Will Your Church Be More Serious About Thanksgiving Celebration?

How serious is your church when it comes to Thanksgiving Day celebration? Unfortunately, we see churches celebrate Thanksgiving Day, and let it pass without any serious thought and emphasis on its purpose and in the Word of God. It's good to have pumpkin and turkey. It's great to have some church dinner and music, but it also must be Christ centered. The church must be focus on the Lord Jesus Christ, and what He has done on the cross for our salvation. I am not against any of those banqueting, parties, thanksgiving concert, and other related thanksgiving celebrations; but God expect us to honor His name, and if possible or if the Lord will open the door of opportunity; be sure to share the good news of salvation. Of course, we assume that the main object and purpose of everything that we are doing on Thanksgiving Day was for His glory. The Bible says; "17-And whatsoever ye do in word or deed, do all in the name of the Lord Jesus, giving thanks to God and the Father by him. 23- And whatsoever ye do, do it heartily, as to the Lord, and not unto men;" (Colossians 3:17, 23 KJV) Help your church celebrate Thanksgiving Day with a "Kingdom focus" attitude of gratitude.

Thanksgiving could be God's given occasion to the church for the purpose of sharing the Lord's death, burial and resurrection. The reason behind it is because people will usually visit church with Christian love ones the day before Thanksgiving Day to thank God for His goodness. The Sunday after Thanksgiving Day could be a day where family who visits will come together to church for worship. Some of the family members of our brothers and sisters in Christ are unsaved. We need to grab the opportunity to share the Word of God. Remember they are in the stages of being pious in a way... and religious in their mind set within the week. I do not suggest to take off the fun in the celebration, but to add the more needful, and the most important part of celebrating thanksgiving. Even King Solomon, King David, and Apostle Paul in their gratefulness, and expression of gratitude to the goodness and mercy of God did not set aside the Word of God. Instead, they put God and His Word in the frontline. God is always the reason for the good and godly celebrations. It should always be centered on Him and about Him. Although some people here at home and those from the other side of the world commercialized Thanksgiving Day, believers should spiritualized it. Spiritualize it in a way where we could share the good news of salvation in some ways.

What pastors John Lindongan of Bukidnon, Philippines, Joe Hurst of Hawaii, and Eliezer Dumala Sagansay of International Community Christian Church in Trenton, Michigan are doing on those special days are the good example of using the celebrations for a good and Christ centered purpose. We will talk more about what these ministers are doing in their respective ministries on the next chapters.

HOW THE WORLD CELEBRATE THANKSGIVING

We are living in a generation of cultures and changed. People, cultures, traditions, life, and almost everything in this world have changed. But there are some practices, and cultures or traditions that never changed. Thanksgiving Day is one of the celebrations that never changed here in the United States. But let's check out some of the countries from the other side of our world on how they celebrate thanksgiving, and if the attitude of gratitude is a big deal to a changing world.

a) In the Philippines

The attitude of gratitude is a big deal to a country like the Philippines. A son or a daughter who don't pay back their parents after they finished college and get a job may be considered as ungrateful child. The children who made it in life financially, and did not pay back their struggling parents will all be called "ungrateful" children no matter what you have accomplished for the community. Your involvement in any charity will be considered "Just a Show..." If you were once helped by a friend or neighbor in some ways; somehow that neighbor or friend may expect you to pay back, and if you don't; then you will be tagged as ungrateful. Thus; gratefulness, gratitude, and being thankful is indeed a big deal to many Filipinos.

A pastor from the Philippines was talking to me about thanksgiving, and he was sharing to me about how he was thankful to God for his life. He was thankful to God for being useful to God in spite of his old age and physical weakness. You may have heard of people who almost have everything this life can offer; but they complain of the things this life could not offer them. Gratefulness is not about what you have, but what you may not have as well.

Reverend John Lindongan is from Malaybalay, Bukidnon but he is now based in Northridge, California. Pastor John shared to me how they celebrate thanksgiving in their church in California as well as how they do it in his hometown in Malaybalay, Bukidnon in Mindanao, Philippines. He said; "This special occasion (Thanksgiving Day) is celebrated on last week of October until first Sunday of November." Obviously, it's observed on a different days and month. October in the Philippines is "Semestral Break" of the students, especially those who are in college of which many of the students in some Christian churches would take part on such occasion. Pastor John said that the last Sunday of October is just the start of something bigger. He said, "Food was being served in churches from morning 'til night with in between snacks- all for free. This is open for everyone in the community, even to strangers, and people from other cities visiting their home church, family or community."

"Thanksgiving Day is like a feast for churches", he added. And I wonder how many churches here in the USA and in the other parts of the world have the same attitude and celebrations. Sometimes, due to hardships, and deep financial condition of the churches, the church members were asked to hosts or sponsor for the meals. First Sunday of November is the big celebration in their village. They invite everyone for a feast of food and *good* drinks, he meant non alcoholic. They even invite other religious groups for fellowship. They also have a "Worship Rally" or a "Sunday Rally". It's the time where the mother church will host the daughter churches for a joint worship. The small churches and partners in the ministry will make some contributions for the special "Thanksgiving Worship". He said; "Lechon or roast pig will definitely be a part to end the week long celebrations". On that final Sunday of Thanksgiving Weeks or Months; everyone will be asked to bring all kinds of fruits and vegetables. He explained the reasons why the church members are expected to bring their thanksgiving offering of fruits and vegetables, including sacks of rice or coconut, banana, sugarcane and pineapple. It's heavy and bulky, but they carry those to church. I asked John what the church would do to the fruits and vegetables; he said; "The main speaker will be the fortunate man to pick whatever he wants from the fruits and vegetables that was offered as thanksgiving offering." The rest will be distributed to the members as he elaborated to me the details of what will happen next after the main speaker is gone. Believe it or not, the main speaker has the option to take everything home if he decided to do so. After the main speaker, the senior pastor will pick his portion and then the church members who may have an interest with the thanksgiving offering. Pastor John was given the opportunity to be the thanksgiving speaker in a church in Malaybalay, Bukidnon. And I will not let anybody know what he picked, and how much fruits and vegetables he took home that day.

Lighthouse Fundamental Baptist Church is in Pat Pat Malaybalay City, Bukidnon, Philippines. Johnsley Lindongan is the pastor of the church with more than a hundred in attendance. They celebrated thanksgiving on September 12, 2012 with roast pigs, chickens, fruits and vegetables. It's out of the traditional date of American Thanksgiving Day. But will it be an issue to other religions? What if they celebrate thanksgiving in a different way? I don't think that would be an issue because I believe thanksgiving to God's children is an every day attitude and practice. We don't have to be tied on its date. Apostle Paul wrote; "But now, after that ye have known God, or rather are known of God, how turn ye again to the weak and beggarly elements, whereunto ye desire again to be in bondage? Ye observe days, and months, and times, and years…" (Colossians 2:8- 16; Galatians 4:9- 10 KJV) Also in II Corinthians 1:11 it says; "as you also join in helping us by prayer, so that many people may give thanks to God for the gracious gift given to us through the help of many." It's all about being thankful to God in His grace and goodness.

Pastor John used the celebration to invite people to church and he tied it up to evangelism. He offered food for people to enjoy, and pushed it with the preaching of the Word of God for the lost souls. He had people who came from different walks of life during the celebration. But it's nothing compared to what they were doing a long time ago due to its longevity and preparations. It used to be a long celebration until life becomes tougher to many farmers and business people. We believe that thanksgiving should not just be a celebration and preparations, but a consistent practice or lifestyle. Pastor John said that "Thanksgiving Day" in Mindanao was introduced by the American missionaries a long time ago with worship and fellowship. But the Filipino pastors and churches made it more memorable and Grande. The Philippines has more than 7,107 islands, with more than 80 dialects, and different cultures; so what you may experience in Mindanao could be different in the western or northern parts of the country.

We know that even during the time of Moses; they celebrated thanksgiving in their own way of saying thanks to God, and singing praises to His name for their deliverance. My wife shared to me the way they celebrated thanksgiving when she was a little girl in her hometown. She said, they used to celebrate thanksgiving after a good harvest in their small farm. The Bible says that we are one in the Lord, and we must stand together in unity whether in pain, in sorrow, in good times, and in bad times. We must stand together for God with thanksgiving in our hearts. We are the salt and light of the darkened world of which being grateful is an inward and outward expresion of being a Christian.

b) In China and Japan

You will be surprise to know that the Japanese people don't celebrate Thanksgiving Day. According to my Japanese friend; "Japan has always been Japan since then." She said; "Japan was never been influenced by any culture or power." A Chinese friend said that New Year is big in China, and in the Chinese community all over the world, but he don't remember celebrating thanksgiving day in Hong Kong or mainland China as big as Chinese New Year's Day. Of course you don't have to be under the influence of power, another country or culture and traditions to celebrate such occasion. We can and we must always be thankful, every day, anytime, anywhere, and in any situations, conditions, and circumstances that we are in. And it doesn't have to be big.

c) In Cambodia and Canada

My son's fiancée is Cambodian- American. Judy's parents were from Cambodia, but Judy was born in Michigan, USA. I asked Judy if she remember celebrating Thanksgiving Day the Cambodian way or in Cambodian culture and tradition. She said; "Not that I know of..." I asked my friend from Windsor, Canada how they as a family and as a church celebrate thanksgiving. He said, "We celebrate Thanksgiving Day similar on how the US celebrates the occasion." And my good friend pastor Andy Sarmiento shared to me the same perspective as Joe Hurst in their way of celebrating Thanksgiving Day. An individual with Christ in his or her heart will have the same outlook and perspective when it comes to spreading the good news and our salvation in Christ. They will use the occasions, the situations, the institutions, the corporations, and anything that they can think of with the intention to share Jesus to the lost world.

HOW THE CHURCHES
CELEBRATE THANKSGIVING

"Thankful for what…?" That's one of the questions of the ungrateful people. Remember: *Never Complain About Anything!* Apostle Paul wrote; "11- Not that I speak in respect of want: for I have learned, in whatsoever state I am, therewith to be content. 12- I know both how to be abased, and I know how to abound: everywhere and in all things I am instructed both to be full and to be hungry, both to abound and to suffer need. 13- I can do all things through Christ which strengtheneth me." (Philippians 4:11- 13 KJV)

One day while I was walking down to my room in Ramada Hotel few hours before our "Ramada Worship Night". Behind me was the group of hockey team- the children who visited Taylor, Michigan for a game. I was not nosey on their conversations, but I overheard one of the remarks of the little boy. He said, "I hate this hotel, I hate this place, and I don't want to stay in this place." If you are in a carpeted hotel, with swimming pools, gym, spa, game room, Television set with cable and Internet; how can you hate such place? I would not be surprise on the attitudes of some of the children who don't know what it means to be poor, who don't know anything about poverty, who've never seen people living in shanties or living with nothing but pillows and roof or nothing at all.

In 2007, we went to the Philippines for a vacation. You know how expensive it would be for the whole family to go together, but it helps turned my children's heart with a better perspective, and they begin to appreciate what we have here in the States. They never have any clue what life is in that beautiful country. They get to have the feel, and they realized what it means to be poor after that visit. Some of the children thought that to be poor for them means you don't have the leisure, luxuries, and pleasures of the rich. One day my son EJ said; "We're very poor, because we don't have a nice and expensive car, and our house is not as big as my friend's house!" People will complain of what they don't have, and will also complain of what they have, but they want more or better. Some has the reason to complain but some would find some reasons to complain.

Contentment, satisfaction, gratefulness, and to be happy of what you have is, I believe the key to this kind of attitude. Remember that "Only Jesus Can Satisfy Your Soul". When Apostle Paul wrote this verse; "In everything give thanks: for this is the will of God in Christ Jesus concerning you." (I Thessalonians 5:18) He was not living in luxury or staying in a five star hotel. He was in fact in a dungeon. He did not have the freedom and the material blessings that we enjoy. He could be in a worst situation my mind could ever imagine. "Never Complain About Anything at Anytime"

"Thankful for what...? You Want Me to Say Thank You for This...?" I heard it all the time from all kinds of people, and from all walks of life. The words of Tertullus may be out of context to use about being grateful and thankful to others.

We must be aware that millions of people are not in the same boat with us as Christians. But I believe Tertullus has a point when he said; "We accept it always, and in all places, most noble Felix, with all thankfulness." (Acts 24:3 KJV) Their religious belief might be different, their philosophy in life could be twisted, and in opposite to your upbringing and culture. Or they may have different principles from yours, but to appreciate the good deeds of others will not hurt, and twist your arms to what they believe in. The question should not be "Thankful for What…?" but "What Else Should I Thank God For…"

A conservative pastor was outraged to his fellow pastor because the later publicly recognized and appreciated the "job well done" by the minister of the other religion. It is not wrong to appreciate the unbelievers or ministers of other religious group if they have done something good and exemplary. If everyone will have a positive and thankful attitude toward those who made an accomplishment, and worthy endeavors; we would not have problems with envy, jealousy, and crab mentality. If you study the attitude of the crabs when placed in a bucket, they pull each other down when one of them is making its way up to the top. It's very common to some countries. The ungrateful and negative person will likely overlook the good things, the good deeds, or the great accomplishment by good people.

The United States of America is a land of the free, and we enjoy the freedom as well as the abundance of our land. Our children enjoy the good education that they got from this great country. We have opportunities that other countries couldn't give or offer to their citizenry. We have equality, and we can walk in the mall, at the store or anywhere we want, and not be discriminated because of the color of our skin or because we have a different accent. And the awesome thing about America is its freedom of expression or speech, and the religious freedom that we have. We can sleep peacefully in the middle of the night, and not be worried of the government knocking in our doors because we exercised our religion somewhere or in our own home. It means in public worship and in private worship. This is one of the blessings that other countries in the world don't have, and can't have for now. Millions have to go underground to sing praises to our God or to worship Him in spirit and in truth. I'm always reminding my church and children of the blessing of the religious freedom that we have in this country. Christians and other religious groups should be thankful about it. I don't know if those who were from afar who came here in America have ever been thinking of the bountiful blessings or freedom of speech that we have and freely enjoy.

JESUS ON THANKSGIVING (LUKE 17:16)

Would Jesus be on Thanksgiving?

Yes, He did and He will. Jesus will surely teach and preach about thanksgiving if He is with us physically right now! In the book of Luke 17:1- 9; Jesus shared to His disciples the story about the Good Samaritan. In Luke 17:10- 19; Jesus healed the unthankful and the grateful lepers that He met on the road. Jesus set an example for us to follow.

I.   He Gave Thanks for the Cup- (Matthew 26:27)

II.   He Gave Thanks for the Bread- (Mark 14:21- 26)

III.   He Gave Thanks for the Enemy- (Luke 6:32)

IV.   He Gave Thanks for the Unlovable- (Luke 6:31- 32)

V.   He Gave Thanks for the Sinners, but Not the Sin. (Luke 31- 33)

VI.   He Gave Thanks for the Lender Who Don't Pay… (Luke 6:34- 35)

VII.   He Gave Thanks for the Ungrateful Enemies, Lender, and Sinners… (Luke 6:34- 36)

VIII.   He is Kind to the Unthankful. (Luke 6:36)

IX.   He Wants Us to Thank Him for Our Service to Our Lord and King. (Luke 17:7- 10)

X.   He Thank the Father for Hearing Him. (John 11:41)

We can be thankful in a wrong way and with a wrong motive. We can even be thankful in a selfish way. I heard a story about a man who was so thankful because during the storm, and the flood everyone was affected and their crops were damaged but his fields were untouched, and nothing unusual happened to him and his family. It's not wrong to be thankful to God if nothing bad or evil comes our way while others are suffering, but the best thing to do is to utter, and give God the praise and the honor in private. But we have to pray for the victims both in our private prayer or personal devotion as well as in our public prayer. You cry with those who cry and laugh with those who laugh. Jesus shared a story to His disciples in Luke 18:9- 14 about the praying Publican and Pharisee. This is a beautiful parable about these two religious gentlemen who went to the temple to pray. The Bible says; "9- And he spake this parable unto certain which trusted in themselves that they were righteous, and despised others: 10- Two men went up into the temple to pray; the one a Pharisee, and the other a publican. 11- The Pharisee stood and prayed thus with himself, God, I thank thee, that I am not as other men are, extortioners, unjust, adulterers, or even as this publican. 12- I fast twice in the week, I give tithes of all that I possess. 13- And the publican, standing afar off, would not lift up so much as his eyes unto heaven, but smote upon his breast, saying, God be merciful to me a sinner. 14- I tell you, this man went down to his house justified rather than the other: for every one that exalteth himself shall be abased; and he that humbleth himself shall be exalted." (Luke 18:9- 14 KJV)

We can be proud and arrogant with what we have, and who we are. Or we can be as simple and humble as we can be.

It's heartbreaking to watch people live in poverty and sin. It's also heartbreaking to watch those who made it in life and became ungrateful to God. And we observed those who have been helped to stepped up to the top, but in spite of the good things in life, they ignore the goodness of God and others. Some people are successful and wealthy, but they turned their heart from God. The worst thing is some of them not only denied God, but they even make fun of God and Christians. Some of them are arrogant, and have committed the sin of sacrilege. They used God, and the Bible for their own benefits or advantage. A Pharisee during Jesus' times is like those people of this present time who are self righteous, self centered and selfish. I believe they are also unthankful, ungrateful, and are living like the praying Pharisee. Gratefulness and arrogance are words that don't match and don't go together. Ungrateful people are proud and high minded. *Give and be Thankful.* A song popularized by Mr. Don Moen, written by Smith, Henry says;

"Give thanks with a grateful heart,
Give thanks to the Holy One
Give thanks because He's given Jesus Christ, His Son..."

It was God who first gave us everything we need. We can go back from the eternity past when God the Father, the Lord Jesus Christ, and the Holy Spirit saw the need of humanity after the fall. The holy trinity opened the heaven's gates for the salvation of men through the death of the Lord Jesus Christ. It was on eternity past when God planned and provided the needs of men during His creations for six days. He set the seventh day to make it holy which would be another God's show of love and generosity to the sinful humanity.

THE IMPORTANCE OF
THANKSGIVING EVERY DAY

Is it About the Tradition or
American Culture?

A good friend said; "We celebrate thanksgiving because that's our tradition here in America..." Americans celebrate thanksgiving on last Thursday of November. I agree it's our tradition, and we appreciate the settlers as well as Mr. Abraham Lincoln for making it a national holiday and celebration. But it's not just about tradition and culture. Apostle Paul in I Corinthians 14:14- 19 rebuked the church about their attitude toward prayer, praise and speaking of tongues. He said; "14- For if I pray in an unknown tongue, my spirit prayeth, but my understanding is unfruitful. 15- What is it then? I will pray with the spirit, and I will pray with the understanding also: I will sing with the spirit, and I will sing with the understanding also. 16- Else when thou shalt bless with the spirit, how shall he that occupieth the room of the unlearned say Amen at thy giving of thanks, seeing he understandeth not what thou sayest? 17- For thou verily givest thanks well, but the other is not edified. 18- I thank my God, I speak with tongues more than ye all: 19- Yet in the church I had rather speak five words with my understanding, that by my voice I might teach others also, than ten thousand words in an unknown tongue." (1 Corinthians 14:14- 19 KJV). Apostle Paul emphasized 3 things about the giving of thanks of the brethren: 1) - *Understanding* in verses 15- 17. 2) - *Edification* in verses 17- 18 and, 3) - *Teaching* in verse 19.

We need to know the tradition, the culture and also the spiritual significance of thanksgiving. It's good to know that families, churches and our country celebrate thanksgiving once a year; but we should not confine ourselves and confined the celebration on a certain date, or in a tradition and culture. Let us be flexible in our celebrations. We should know why we must be thankful to God. We must know the impact of our gracefulness and gratefulness to our children and to others. We must believe that thanksgiving is not just about ourselves but for others to be encouraged, and to help them in their present difficult situations. People should understand why you are thankful. It must edify the saints and instruct our children. The people around us must know the importance of thanksgiving. We need to teach them the proper way and the right way of celebrating thanksgiving, and how to express their gracefulness, and appreciation for this life in spite of the bad economy, in the midst of chaos, and confusion. Others celebrate thanksgiving in a shameful and sinful way. Thanksgiving must be a time or a day of honor, and praise to our holy God.

Focus on God and His Goodness

The Psalmists' Testimony of Praise and Thanksgiving! King David at the Temple said; "O give thanks unto the

Lord; for he is good; for his mercy endureth for ever."
(1 Chronicles 16:34 KJV)

David recognized and declared in public the goodness of the Lord. We seldom see and hear government officials, and leaders telling their constituents to be thankful to God and give Him praise for His goodness and mercy upon us. There's no question about the ungratefulness of some in spite of all the benefits that they received from the government. But to King David; he was not ashamed to tell his people of what God is doing in his life and in the nation- Israel. Notice what he said in the Scriptures; "12-Remember his marvellous works that he hath done, his wonders, and the judgments of his mouth; 13- O ye seed of Israel his servant, ye children of Jacob, his chosen ones. 24- Declare his glory among the heathen; his marvellous works among all nations." (1 Chronicles 16:12, 13, 24 KJV) How I wish every leaders of the land will have the same mind set, and perspective in their respective country, people and to God.

Why David was Grateful

- God is Gracious
- God is Righteous
- God is Merciful
- God is the One Who Preserved Us
  - He Helps Us
  - He is Our Rest
- He Dealt Bountifully with Us
- He Delivered Us: from Death, from Tears, and from Falling,

- For Our Salvation
- For Our Benefits

"5- Gracious is the Lord, and righteous; yea, our God is merciful. 6- The Lord preserveth the simple: I was brought low, and he helped me. 7- Return unto thy rest, O my soul; for the Lord hath dealt bountifully with thee. 8- For thou hast delivered my soul from death, mine eyes from tears, and my feet from falling. 9- I will walk before the Lord in the land of the living. 10- I believed, therefore have I spoken: I was greatly afflicted: 11- I said in my haste, All men are liars. 12- What shall I render unto the Lord for all his benefits toward me? 13- I will take the cup of salvation, and call upon the name of the Lord. 14- I will pay my vows unto the Lord now in the presence of all his people. 15- Precious in the sight of the Lord is the death of his saints. 16- O Lord, truly I am thy servant; I am thy servant, and the son of thine handmaid: thou hast loosed my bonds. 17- I will offer to thee the sacrifice of thanksgiving, and will call upon the name of the Lord. 18- I will pay my vows unto the Lord now in the presence of all his people, 19- In the courts of the Lord's house, in the midst of thee, O Jerusalem. Praise ye the Lord." (Psalms 116:5-19 KJV)

King Solomon and the Dedication of the Temple (I Kings 7:48- 51)

In the book of I Kings chapter eight; King Solomon blessed the Lord and gave praises to His holy name. He also offered and dedicated all kinds of precious stones, gold and jewels to God. King Solomon worshipped and praised the Lord with thanksgiving in his heart by giving back to God what He deserved.

Moses in Exodus (Exodus 15:1- 4)

"1- Then sang Moses and the children of Israel this song unto the LORD, and spake, saying, I will sing unto the LORD, for he hath triumphed gloriously: the horse and his rider hath he thrown into the sea. 2- The LORD is my strength and song, and he is become my salvation: he is my God, and I will prepare him an habitation; my father's God, and I will exalt him. 3- The LORD is a man of war: the LORD is his name. 4- Pharaoh's chariots and his host hath he cast into the sea: his chosen captains also are drowned in the Red sea." It was a celebration of thanksgiving and praise for what God has done.

The whole chapter of Daniel six is a story about Daniel and his miraculous experienced with God in spite of his persecution, and in spite of those who tried to stop him from praying. Some politicians in the political arena are rediculed for their corruption or scandals, but Daniel was rediculed, persecuted, and was thrown in the lions den for his conviction, for his love for God, and because he stood up for the truth of the Word of God. But with all of the negative experiences that he went through; Daniel was thankful and he gave thanks to God. The Bible says; "10- Now when Daniel knew that the writing was signed, he went into his house; and his windows being open in his chamber toward Jerusalem, he kneeled upon his knees three times a day, and prayed, and gave thanks before his God, as he did aforetime. 11- Then these men assembled, and found Daniel praying and making supplication before his God. 12- Then they came near, and spake before the king concerning the king's decree; Hast thou not signed a decree, that every man that shall ask a petition of any God or man within thirty days, save of thee, O king, shall be cast into the den of lions? The king answered and said, The thing is true, according to the law of the Medes and Persians, which altereth not." (Daniel 6:10- 12)

APOSTLE PAUL IN JAIL WITH A GRATEFUL HEART, AND HIS ATTITUDE OF GRATITUDE (ACTS 16:22- 28)

I.   Paul was Thankful for the Dedicated Christians and Churches. (Romans 16:4)

II. Paul was Thankful for the Grace of God. (I Corinthians 1:4)

III. Paul was Thankful for the Victory through Our Lord Jesus Christ. (I Corinthians 15:57)

IV. Paul was Thankful for Titus and His Care for the Christians and Churches. (II Corinthians 8:16- 17)

V.   Paul Wants 'Giving of Thanks…' be Named Among Christians and Churches (Ephesians 5:3- 4)

VI. Paul was Thankful for the Christians… (Colossians 1:3; 3:15; I Thessalonians 1:2; 3:9; 5:18)

VII. Paul was Thankful for the Uncontrolled Negative Circumstances in Life. (Acts 28:1- 15)

THE UNGRATEFUL PEOPLE ARE...

Unhappy

In the malls, at the airports, in the bus stations, in a fancy hotels and restaurants, in the banks, and even in a mansions and palaces; we see and heard of unhappy people. What's wrong with our world? Whatever happened to the beautiful malls, and the comfort of flying and travelling from point "A" to point "B" and not be worried that we will be the next Titanic disaster victims is a question that the unthankful and unhappy person can answer. I would rather be standing in line waiting for my turn to board in a bus, a boat or a plane than walking or riding in a Philippine buffalo or a horse. I heard people complain in a fancy restaurant while millions of people will go to bed at night with empty stomach. I remember those days when I was a little kid, when I would go to the back of the restaurant and asked the waiters or the chef for the leftovers. Sometimes, we would wait for the restaurant to close in the middle of the night so we could get all the leftovers that could look like a swine's food already.

In a tennis club where I grew up working as a ball boy; I remember waiting with other kids until the middle of the night for the club members to leave so we could feast on the leftovers. God has blessed me with so much that it's time for me to share His blessings. Now, I don't have to worry waiting for the leftovers. I'm so thankful to God just to be alive and well. Whatever I have on the table, I can't complain. My children used to complain every time they get home from school or work when they open the refrigerator and don't see what they wanted to eat. They would always say; "There's nothing to eat, we have no food…" What they actually mean- they don't see the food they wanted to eat. In spite of the abundance of food and drinks, they complain. They complain that we have no more cereals when what they actually mean is, they don't see their favorite cereals. It was until we went to the Philippines and witnessed what it means to have nothing on the table. *Nothing* in some of the homes means an empty house. They saw the real poverty and hunger in the street children's face. They saw some homes don't even have a refrigerator or television. It changed their perspective in life. My children are now thankful and grateful. I didn't hear them complain since that visit. The third world countries don't have the pleasure of having what the rich countries such as the United States have, but you would be surprise- they're a happy people. Happiness is not on what you have, and what you have obtained; it's in being happy and grateful to God for it. Have you notice some of the people who made it in life? They are successful in their life and career, but they're not happy. Why? It's because of their discontentment and ungratefulness in life.

Unfulfilled Life

What can make us a fulfilled individual? Who and what makes a person fulfilled? Is fulfillment based on accomplishment? Is wealth the answer to fulfillment? Can we find fulfillment in our worldly possessions?

A man was talking to his friend about his new grandson said; "yes, I felt like I'm a fulfilled man." He was asked by his friend why and what made him conclude he was a fulfilled person? People could think that way, but how can you gauge a person if he or she is fulfilled? Can you tell who is fulfilled and who's not? For me, one thing for sure; I believe that the unfulfilled persons are the ungrateful or unthankful people in spite of God's blessings. God can give us true fulfillment and fill our empty soul. One of the things that we can be sure of as believers is we have true fulfillment with Jesus in our hearts. A person who is living an unfulfilled life is living with ungrateful or unthankful life. Jesus said; "9- I am the door: by me if any man enter in, he shall be saved, and shall go in and out, and find pasture. 10- The thief cometh not, but for to steal, and to kill, and to destroy: I am come that they might have life, and that they might have it more abundantly." (John 10:9- 10 KJV) We must trust the Lord in our unfulfilled life, unfulfilled dreams, unfulfilled goals, and let us be thankful to God even if we don't feel fulfilled.

Dissatisfied Life

King David knew that if Jesus is your Shepherd, it means you have satisfaction, and you will not live in want. King David said; "1- The LORD is my shepherd; I shall not want. 2-He maketh me to lie down in green pastures: he leadeth me beside the still waters. 3- He restoreth my soul:

he leadeth me in the paths of righteousness for his name's sake." (Psalm 23:1- 3 KJV) The world are not satisfied even if they're inspired, they may not be gratified, because they live a life dissatisfied…

Discontent Life

Contentment is the word that's missing in many homes and workplaces. Conflicts triggered because of discontentment. Apostle Paul said; "6- But godliness with contentment is great gain. 7- For we brought nothing into this world, and it is certain we can carry nothing out. 8- And having food and raiment let us be therewith content." (I Timothy 6:6- 8 KJV) For me; I am very happy, grateful, and content to be alive and well. In the midst of my personal storms, my personal roller coaster rides, and in spite of conflicting stairways to my final destination; the attitude of gratitude must be exercise with contentment. It's absolutely true that if an individual is unthankful, he or she will be discontent, dissatisfied, double minded, and most of the time discourage. These are the people who are drifting in their walk with God. They will have an unstable and wavering faith in God. The Bible said; "4- But let patience have her perfect work, that ye may be perfect and entire, wanting nothing. 5- If any of you lack wisdom, let him ask of God, that giveth to all men liberally, and upbraideth not; and it shall be given him. 6- But let him ask in faith, nothing wavering. For he that wavereth is like a wave of the sea driven with the wind and tossed. 7- For let not that man think that he shall receive any thing of the Lord. 8- A double minded man is unstable in all his ways." (James 1:4- 8 KJV)

"THANK YOU" (WE SAY IT ALL THE TIME!)

I was in Manila, Philippines for a mission trip with my wife. Our host pastor Benny Bernal was so gracious and generous to always take us out for the whole day for meals. One morning, pastor Bernal took us to a popular fast food restaurant in Manila. As we were waiting for our orders until we ate and left; I observed that the security guard who welcomes the customers and guests of the restaurant was so busy welcoming, opening, and closing the door for the customers who come and go. But what actually caught my attention was his some kind of a "scripted phrases". The security guard would always say; "Welcome to..." And for those who would leave or comes out of the restaurant, he would say; "Thank you ma'am, thank you sir, please come again..." And it did not matter if the customers were decent or look like a bum. It did not matter if they were young or old or a high school student. He addressed everyone with respect or with Filipino courtesy and hospitality. Watching him saying the same thing to different kinds of people compels me to come near him, and asked him this question; "How many times did you say 'Thank You' to people the whole time you're here during your shift?" I was looking at his face and in his eyes; he was kind of surprise, and was in disbelief that someone would ask him such question. He said; "Ahh, Ahh… Why do you ask me such question, sir?" I said; "I'm writing about thanksgiving and I wanted to feature you on my next project." He quickly answered; "Between five hundred to a thousand, and it depends if we're slow or doing well. On holidays and pay days; we're really busy, it means more 'Thank you' to say during those days." I made a follow up question as I looked at him straight to his eyes; "Do you really mean it when you say; 'Welcome... And, thank you'?" He answered with confidence; "Yes sir". I asked; "What made you say that you really mean it?" He said; "Because we were taught to mean it, because people will know it if I don't really mean it." The security guard added; "Sir, the customers are smart, and they can tell by your voice or gestures if you don't mean what you say". That could be a good lesson to learn; you always say "Thank you" and mean it?

I'm sure you have been greeted by a friend, love ones, co-workers or someone down the road with these words; "Hello, how are you?" or "What's up?" "Are you alright?" They are the people who tried or wanted to be nice to you. But someone from the United Kingdom asked me this question; "Do you Americans really mean it when you say; Hello, How are you?" Or "What's up?" We can ask the same question in response to those who asked or greeted us with a good and right motive. Do we really mean it when we say; "I'm good" "I'm doing well" "I'm fine, thank you". It's something that we need to practice from the heart. It's the same way for the people with a thankful heart. They mean it, and it's from the heart. My African-American friend was sharing to me about his experienced in greeting a tourist at the Park. He greeted the tourist; "Good Morning, what's up?" To my friend's surprise, the tourist responded; "Good Morning!" and made a respectful gesture by looking up. The tourist may have a different understanding of the words; "What's up?" Or the tourist may have meant "Thank you" to God when he looked up or it may meant something else for the tourist. But being thankful is the right thing to do!

But, Are We Grateful?

I was in Temecula, California for a church planting and mission work. I asked the Lord as I prayed the night before to send a soul in my path for me to share His love and grace. The following day the Lord answered my prayer. He sent a homeless man who was so scary to look upon. When I saw him coming to where I was seated, I honestly was thinking of standing up and walk away. But I was stopped by the Holy Spirit, and I stayed seated waiting for the homeless man to come. I expected him to ask for money or something, but I was wrong. The man was so nice and he did not ask for anything. He was courteous, respectful and smart. I gave him my water, chips, and sandwiches but he refused and I insist. He shared to me how he lost his health when he injured himself in an accident. Because of his disability, he lost his business, and got a divorce from his wife of about 20 years. His children don't care about him. His friends and relatives rejected him and turned their back on him when he became homeless. But I was amazed to hear from this homeless man when he said; "I'm thankful to God for this life and for just being alive and well". Can you imagine that kind of attitude? Can you be thankful when you don't have your own house, your own bathroom, your own table, your own chairs and plates on the table? He didn't know where to get his next meals? It's so sad and unfortunate to hear people complain of a hot room, a cold dining room, or a cold meal while others don't own a pillow or a plate. Are you grateful today?

How About the Timing and the Situations?

Is it normal to say "Thank you Lord" in spite of difficulties, and tough times in life? How about if you're going through tough times, and in an uncontrolled circumstances? Those are some of the questions of people who heard some God loving, and dedicated Christians making positive remarks in spite of sufferings and trials in life. The lost world will not understand the positive attitude of Christians in the midst of the storms in life. People may question the negative remarks and attitude, but not the positive. People should be surprised of the wrong and bad attitudes. The right and the good attitude must not be in question.

FAMILY DEVOTIONAL FOR THANKSGIVING DAY

Value God's Blessings

"9- And Jabez was more honourable than his brethren: and his mother called his name Jabez, saying, Because I bare him with sorrow. 10- And Jabez called on the God of Israel, saying, Oh that thou wouldest bless me indeed, and enlarge my coast, and that thine hand might be with me, and that thou wouldest keep me from evil, that it may not grieve me! And God granted him that which he requested." (I Chronicles 4:9- 10)

The Lord's blessings may come our way in different forms. I asked my group 2 different questions one day: 1- If they have prayed for God's blessings that day and everybody raised their hands. 2- How many of you asked the Lord for a specific blessing? Nobody raised their hand. We asked God for general blessings but forgot to thank Him for one small thing. We expect God to do some miracles for us, and we overlooked to thank Him for the little things that we enjoyed. Jabez prayed, "…Oh that thou wouldest bless me indeed" We have general blessings, but we also have individual, and special blessings. The problem is, we sometimes don't take pleasures and value with what God has given us. Value God's blessing, value your family, your love ones with you, and the freedom to serve the Lord. You are being used by God for His kingdom. Do you know what it means to be away from home for a long time, and what it means to have a death in the family? How about the pain of watching a family member leaves for some reasons? Others don't have any idea how it would feel to be financially distress. Others don't know the feelings of going to bed with empty stomach. Others are suffering with health issues in spite of their love for God and their family. Some are abusing their bodies with alcohol, cigarettes and drugs… and were unthankful to God. Sometimes people are only thankful on special holidays. Notice one of my favorite hymns:

"When upon life's billows you are tempest tossed, when you are discouraged, thinking all is lost, Count your many blessings, name them one by one, And it will surprise you what the Lord hath done. Count your blessings, name them one by one, Count your blessings, see what God hath done! Count your blessings, name them one by one, And it will surprise you what the Lord hath done. So, amid the conflict whether great or small, Do not be disheartened, God is over all; Count your many blessings, angels will attend, Help and comfort give you to your journey's end." (Johnson Oatman Jr., by Edwin Excell (Chicago, Illinois: 1897).

What do you think was in Jabez's mind when he prayed that prayer? How do you value the Lord's blessings in your life? Which of the following are more valuable to you: 1) God- and why? 2) Family- and why? 3) Friends- and Why? 4) The Holy Bible- and why? 5) Work or ministry- and why? 6) Wealth, integrity or dignity and why? 7) Others, and why? If God's blessings are valuable to you, will you share it to others?

"After the Big Thanksgiving Celebration… What?"

"1- O come, let us sing unto the LORD: let us make a joyful noise to the rock of our salvation. 2- Let us come before his presence with thanksgiving, and make a joyful noise unto him with psalms." (Psalm 95:1- 2)

If we have after Christmas sale, after Christmas best deals, after Christmas sales tips and the after Christmas clean ups. After Christmas check and balance of credit cards debt, and the check and balance of our bank account. Checking on how much you've gain or lose because of so much food and stress. But remember to keep the Spirit of Christmas in our hearts. The Christmas celebration is on December 25, but the Spirit of Christmas must be 24/7, 365 or 366 days a year. Don't leave the Spirit of Christmas on the table, in your unwrapped gifts or in your Christmas tree. Keep it in your hearts as you keep the Lord's commandment. We can keep the Spirit of Christmas with God's love, and our devotion to Him and Him alone. And think of the same scenario as that of Christmas as you celebrate Thanksgiving Day. Let His Spirit, God's Spirit dwell in *you*. We must also remember on the other hand of the spirit of true Thanksgiving Day Celebrations. Think of the same ideas on Thanksgiving Day; what's next *after the big Thanksgiving Day…?*

Be Generous, It's Your Way of Saying; "Thank You Lord"

"5- Thou preparest a table before me in the presence of mine enemies: thou anointest my head with oil; my cup runneth over. 6- Surely goodness and mercy shall follow me all the days of my life: and I will dwell in the house of the LORD forever." (Psalms 23:5- 6)

I love this beautiful story with full of spiritual lessons. It's about the 2 boys who were best friends for a long time. They have 2 different personalities, characters and attitudes. Friend number 1 was a good, nice, selfless and positive boy. We may say he's almost perfect in his attitude, lifestyle, character, moral value, and his outlook in life. Boy number 1 was a generous and compassionate kind of individual. But boy number 2 was the opposite. He was a bad, selfish and negative boy. He spent his life for his own and he didn't care about others. He has the "I" "Me" "My" attitude. One day as they were walking in the woods… they met an old, old woman. The woman showed them 2 sets of tables with golden spoons, forks, etc. One of the tables was long and everything on it. And the other one were all regular sizes. And the good news was- the woman was giving everything away to the boys. The old woman asked the boy number 1 first to make a choice or pick his table. And to her surprised, boy number 1 turned the opportunity to his friend. Boy number 2 excitedly accepted the offer and he picked the golden long table with all the golden kitchen wares on it. Boy number 2 did not realized that everything they picked would be theirs even after death. You may think… Wow!

That was even great and a great deal too, it's free! No! It was not a good deal and it was not great; because the 12 foot long of spoons, forks, knives, glasses and cups, and the 30 foot long table will be his in eternity. Boy number 2 will eat from those in eternity. How can he feed himself with those long golden table wares? That was the problem, and that's what he got for being selfish, greedy, discontent, and for having the wrong value. Did you notice the difference between the 2 and their destiny? It happens every day all over the globe. People selfishly make bad decisions, and take the temporal more than the eternal.

May we would have the heart like King David who said: "Thou preparest a table before me in the presence of mine enemies…" (Psalms 23:5) Let the Lord shower you with His blessings, and be a channel of those blessings. Let's picture ourselves having the 12 foot long utensils in our hands, and with all the good food on our 30 foot long table; the only requirement was for us to eat using the golden table wares (spoons and forks etc.) to feed ourselves. That would be impossible to feed yourself with those long utensils. The only way for us to be fed is to share one another's food, time, and utensils by feeding one another. As God's children, we let the Lord prepare the table for us. We let Him prepare the blessing before us. Let God prepare the ministry for you. God will not lead us to greener pastures if we are selfish, and if we do not let the good Shepherd lead us. Not only that God's blessing awaits you, but His goodness and mercy will follow you. Notice the testimony of King David when he said; "Thou preparest a table before me in the presence of mine enemies: thou anointest my head with oil; my cup runneth over." (Psalms 23:5) So what do you want to do? Do you want to do it God's way? It means you let Him prepare the table for you. You will let God do the work for you. Or you will let God work in you, and through you by sharing, giving or by being generous, and not being selfish? Are you going to do it your way? It means "I" "ME" "MY" attitude. In (Isaiah 55:8- 9) "8- For my thoughts are not your thoughts, neither are your ways my ways, saith the LORD. 9- For as the heavens are higher than the earth, so are my ways higher than your ways, and my thoughts than your thoughts."

Give- (II Corinthians 8:1- 2) It's not what's in your pocket or bank account, and what you have at home that will make you thankful, but what's in your heart. You have Jesus the Savior of the world. He owns everything. The prince of preacher said; "If you only serve for the applause of men, you sacrifice the approval of God. As Christ's followers, we should not be surprised if the service we render to others in Jesus' name is unappreciated or even spurned." (Charles Haddon Spurgeon)

Keep serving the Lord in spite of... and in the midst of... whether you have blessings or trials. Give! In II Corinthians chapter eight verse one it says; "1- you have the heart for true worship, you will surely learn to serve and give." When Jesus showed Himself to the disciples in different occasions on that resurrection day; it was a blessed day, and a day of joy and blessings. They worship Him, and give themselves to God first. God desires your heart full of gratitude more than anything else... He wants your heart of worship with thanksgiving and praise. In Ephesians chapter five verses nineteen and twenty it says; "Speaking to yourselves in psalms and hymns and spiritual songs, singing and making melody in your heart to the Lord; 20- Giving thanks always for all things unto God and the Father in the name of our Lord Jesus Christ;"

Be Joyful, Sing and Worship the Lord Our God

God's grace enables us to face the music… even when we don't like the tunes. It is possible to have tears in our eyes, while there is song in our heart. That's exactly what David as God's servant went through and said. Songs and singing is not only for good times but also for bad times. Music is not only for time of blessings, but in times of pain and sorrow. People have different reasons for singing. You can sing for money, for fame, to please people, and for your own pleasure, but Christians sings to express our gratefulness to God and to bring honor to His holy name. We sing as an expression of our love and worship to Him. It's easy to do that when you're at church or in a mountain top experience, but it would be a different story if you're in a tough and a rough road. It would be a different story if you're in a situations like Job or Joseph of the Old Testament, and the Apostle Paul when he was in prison. The Bible encourages us to sing and make melody in our heart for God's glory, to be joyful and to rejoice. You need to worship Him and sing for Him…? (Colossians 3:16- 17; 23- 24)

We must give thanks to God

In (II Corinthians 9:15) "Thanks be unto God for his unspeakable gift." (Psalms 30:12) "To the end that my glory may sing praise to thee, and not be silent. O LORD my God, I will give thanks unto thee forever."

We must give thanks to God: 1- Give thanks to God for His unspeakable gifts. 2- Let's be thankful to God for the salvation that God gave us through our Lord Jesus Christ. 3- We can also rejoice and be grateful for the spiritual blessings that He blessed us with. 4- And we can also look forward to the heavenly places which God prepared for those who come to Him in humility of spirit. Paul said that we have His grace and the Lord made us accepted in the beloved. One of the things that we may take for granted is "the redemption through his blood". It was not of money, blood of the animals or of man's way, man's will or man-made salvation; but through His blood. 5- We can also look up to God with gratefulness for the forgiveness of our sins through Jesus Christ. The guilt, the dirty conscience, and burdens are all gone, because we were forgiven. 6- Thank God for the brethren and pray for them. Keep them in your prayers, and be thankful to God for the wisdom and knowledge from above. 7- I'm so thankful to God for being a part of your life by sharing to you the Lord's unspeakable gift, and spiritual blessings through His Words of wisdom. Today, don't hesitate to say, "Thank you… ".

Have you ever thank the Lord for the freedom that we have in Him? We can also be grateful for the freedom of this great nation that we have. You can go to bed and get up in the morning and not be worried of the oppression, political, and religious persecution from the government. We have witnessed the violence, and the riots in some parts of the world. We have turmoil, tribulation and tension on every side. We should be thankful to God for the peace of mind in spite of what's going on in our world today. We have His love and the comfort of the Holy Spirit. My niece prayed over the meal and said; "God is good and God is great, I thank you Lord for the food we eat. Amen" You may have heard of the funny prayers of the little kids like this one, but they're serious about their prayers. One of the girl prayed; "Lord thank you because mom and dad did not fight today." I believe they really mean it. Notice Paul's comforting words; "Blessed be the God and Father of our Lord Jesus Christ, who hath blessed us with all spiritual blessings in heavenly places in Christ:" (Ephesians 2:3)

"*Thank You!*"

"4- Enter into his gates with thanksgiving, and into his courts with praise: be thankful unto him, and bless his name. 5- For the LORD is good; his mercy is everlasting; and his truth endureth to all generations." (Psalm 100: 4- 5)

In our morning worship service before I preach, it is my personal practice or some kind of a personal tradition to just seat off front to pray undisturbed. I meditate, and look forward on *what God would do in our worship*. One Sunday while I have my time with God, I came across to a small gospel tract which has been in my Bible for a long time. And let me share with you what it says:

"Thank You!

We say it so often
-when a waitress gives us good service
-when a customer buys our product
-when someone gives us helping hand
Sometimes we show as well as say our thanks
-when we leave a small tip
-when we send a little gift to a friend or hostess
-when we give that warm, sincere hand-shake

I'd like to show my appreciation to you by telling you something that is of far greater value. It is simply that the greatest gift in the world can be yours for the asking. That gift is the friendship of my best friend-Jesus Christ. He took away my sin and guilt and gives me joy and peace. I serve him with loving obedience and find in Him my life, my hope, my everything! He invites you, 'Come unto me, all ye that labor and are heavy laden, and I will give you rest.' He saves; He keeps; He satisfies! Introducing Him to you is the best way that I can say **Thank you!**" (Faith, Prayer & Tract League, Grand Rapids, MI 49504)

My mother was a very grateful person. She would appreciate everything, and I never heard her complain about something or about someone. She also was a very positive person. Every time my wife gave her something, she would treasure them and take care of them. One day, she came to my wife and showed my wife the beautiful jewelries in her hands and on her neck. And my wife said; "They're beautiful, mom". My mother replied, "thank you" with an accent. She added, "You gave this to me more than a decade ago." What a grateful mother in law. Be grateful in everything.

Apostle Paul said; "In everything give thanks..." It's in everything that we have and we don't have. It's everything from the past, the present, the unknown or dark and hopeless future.

So Much to be Thankful...

"O give thanks unto the LORD; call upon his name: make known his deeds among the people." (Psalm 105: 1)

We have so much to be thankful for... Are you grateful or thankful you're being used by God in some ways? Are you thankful to God your sins are forgiven and you are free? "If the Son therefore shall make you free, ye shall be free indeed." (John 8:36; I John 1:7- 9; Psalms 24:1) God owns everything, what a blessing to know. "A Psalm of David. The earth is the LORD'S, and the fullness thereof; the world, and they that dwell therein." (Deuteronomy 10:14) "Behold, the heaven and the heaven of heavens is the LORD'S thy God, the earth also, with all that therein is." (Psalms 50:10-11; I Chronicles 29:11-12; Haggai 2:8) "The silver is mine, and the gold is mine, saith the LORD of hosts." God owns all the money and wealth of the world including those from the top billionaires and millionaires of our time.

"A thankful heart is not only the greatest virtue, but the parent of all other virtues." Cicero, (www.great-inspirational-quotes.com) I love this classic song; "Thank You Lord for the Trials That Come My Way"

"Thank you, Lord,
for the trials that come my way.
In that way I can grow each day
as I let you lead,
And thank you, Lord,
for the patience those trials bring.
In that process of growing,
I can learn to care.
But it goes against the way
I am to put my human nature down
and let the Spirit take control of all I do.
'Cause when those trials come,
my human nature shouts the thing to do;
and God's soft prompting
can be easily ignored." (Internet at
yahoo- Hymnlyrics.org)

No matter what we're going through and no matter how hard and painful life could be; we must learn to thank God and just be thankful… Someone out there may be going through something that could be *worst* than what you're going through right now. The Bible says; "57- And it came to pass, that, as they went in the way, a certain man said unto him, Lord, I will follow thee whithersoever thou goest. 58- And Jesus said unto him, Foxes have holes, and birds of the air have nests; but the Son of man hath not where to lay his head. 62- And Jesus said unto him, No man, having put his hand to the plow, and looking back, is fit for the kingdom of God." (Luke 9:57- 58; 62) Jesus was homeless when He was here on earth. He did not even own a pillow.

You follow the Lord in spite of difficulties in life and with a grateful heart. In (1 Corinthians 6:17- 20) it says, we have to worship God through our bodies, and yield in His Spirit. When you present your bodies, you don't present to God a dirty, defiled, and obviously dead bodies; you present to God that which is holy, undefiled, and clean bodies. We have to love righteousness and holiness inside out. We must offer our life, and all in the holy temple of God which is our bodies, by giving, and dedicating it to God and God alone. We give and we dedicate our whole lives, our soul to God by our love, and worship. We don't sacrifice our dead body, but our holy life to God. It is a life wherein Christ is living in our soul by faith, which makes the body a living sacrifice as you obey His voice. That is our calling in which God expect of us to be willing to obey and sacrifice. (Galatians 2:20) That was Paul's life, a life that is under the power and authority of God. Paul lived his life not in the flesh, but in the Spirit by which he was conformed in both to the nature and will of God. And remember; you cannot sacrifice even your own body without a grateful heart.

And even our bodies must not be made as the instruments of sin and uncleanness. We were set apart for God, and we were called to live a holy life. We must be willing to obey and be faithful to our calling. No looking back to sin and worldly pleasures. No looking back to the former world and worldly life. We have to follow Christ and walk straight in His path. We have decided to follow Jesus, therefore: "No turning back, no turning back…" Those who don't turn back and those who live a holy life have a heart filled with gratitude for God.

If you really love the Lord, being willing to obey to God's calling for you and the issue of faithfulness would not be a problem. And you will take God seriously! Give your life, talents, and your treasures as your expression of your gratitude to God's goodness and love.

Giving Him Praise and the Glory

"1- A Psalm of David. Bless the LORD, O my soul: and all that is within me, bless his holy name. 2- Bless the LORD, O my soul, and forget not all his benefits:" (Psalms 103:1- 2) In the Book of (Psalms 92:1) "It is a good thing to give thanks unto the LORD, and to sing praises unto thy name, O most High." Also in (Psalms 99:3; 5; 9) "3- Let them praise thy great and terrible name; for it is holy. 5- Exalt ye the LORD our God, and worship at his footstool; for he is holy. 9- Exalt the LORD our God, and worship at his holy hill; for the LORD our God is holy." It means by giving Him thanks not just in the midst of blessing, but even in hardships and in pain or sickness. I like this:

"In some of the thing give thanks…
In something, give thanks…
In good things, give thanks…
In my personal thing, give thanks…

> In worthy thing, give thanks...
> In several things, give thanks...
> In most of the thing, give thanks...
> In God's thing, give thanks...
> In your thing, give thanks...
> In everything, give thanks..."

We have so much to be thankful with or so much to be thankful for... There's a hymn which says, "Count your many blessings and name them one by one..." But we have countless blessings that we can't even name them already. Whatever you have at home, in your office, at church- give God the praise and the glory for it. Sometimes we do things unconscious of the Lord's presence, and not knowing that God have a personal interest on whatever we do, and whatever we have in Him and for Him. And it would always be for His name and for His glory. We have here the Lord's Prayer in John 15:1; 4- 5. It means you give praise to God in everything... "1- Praise ye the LORD. Sing unto the LORD a new song, and his praise in the congregation of saints. 2- Let Israel rejoice in him that made him: let the children of Zion be joyful in their King. 3- Let them praise his name in the dance: let them sing praises unto him with the timbrel and harp." (Psalm 149:1- 3) He was in the dark dungeon and in chained with the jailer watching over him. He was waiting for his trial, and was expecting a death penalty. Some of his friends deserted him, and some of the churches he started did not support him, some did not even dare to visit him, and comfort him. But notice the words of the great Apostle Paul in (Philippians 4:6- 8) "6- Be careful for nothing; but in everything by prayer and supplication with thanksgiving let your requests be made known unto God. 7- And the peace of God, which passeth all understanding, shall keep your hearts and minds through Christ Jesus. 8- Finally, brethren, whatsoever things are true, whatsoever things are honest, whatsoever things are just, whatsoever things are pure, whatsoever things are lovely, whatsoever things are of good report; if there be any virtue, and if there be any praise, think on these things."

Be Grateful

"11- And the LORD spake unto Moses, saying, 12- I have heard the murmurings of the children of Israel: speak unto them, saying, At even ye shall eat flesh, and in the morning ye shall be filled with bread; and ye shall know that I am the LORD your God." (Exodus 16:1- 2)

People all over the world are complaining and murmurings just like the Israelites of old, they always complain or they always have something to complain about. Gratefulness or being thankful is very important in our daily walk with God. Being appreciative or grateful is very important as God's light in this darkened world.

Are we stepping on the Israelites' of old footsteps or pattern of life or are we walking in the path of righteousness? We are in the Lord Jesus Christ's pathway. Be thankful to God for your family, friends and financial condition even if it's not as good as you may have expected it to be. (Psalms 100:3- 5; 105:1- 3) So be thankful to God in all things according to the most grateful man in the New Testament era. Thankfulness, gratefulness, gratitude, "thank you" or "praise God" is not the common words we say when things are not going right and well. Unfortunately, it's not a common vocabulary to many individuals and homes. We may have thousands of things to be thankful for, but we can easily be diverted to complain, and concentrate on little things to complain about. But who will argue with Apostle Paul when he said; *'In everything give thanks...'*? Pastors and preachers must learn to teach their congregations to be grateful to God. Parents and teachers should help their children exercise "gratefulness" at all times. Let us be grateful to God for who we are, what we have, and even for what we don't have. In other words; contentment and satisfaction must be in our systems. It should be in our hearts, in our mind, and in our soul. During my seminary times at the International Baptist Theological College in Manila; we used to have a school Morning devotion at 5:30 sharp. Before the speaker would start the sharing of the Word of God, we would sing this song:

> "Thank you Lord for saving my soul;
> Thank you Lord for making me whole
> Thank you Lord for giving to me,
> Thy great salvation so pure and free."

It was refreshing and encouraging because you would learn to appreciate life as you start your day by meditating on the message of the song.

"1-Praise ye the LORD. O give thanks unto the LORD; for he is good: for his mercy endureth forever. 48- Blessed be the LORD God of Israel from everlasting to everlasting: and let all the people say, Amen. Praise ye the LORD." (Psalm 106:1; 48)

Never Complain About Anything at Anytime

"11- Not that I speak in respect of want: for I have learned, in whatsoever state I am, therewith to be content. 12- I know both how to be abased, and I know how to abound: everywhere and in all things I am instructed both to be full and to be hungry, both to abound and to suffer need. 13- I can do all things through Christ which strengtheneth me." (Philippians 4:11- 13) How do you balance contentment with your present economic, physical and spiritual condition? Do you think Jesus will always make us happy and content in spite of discomfort? (I Peter 5:8- 9)

WORDS OF WISDOM ABOUT THANKSGIVING

When you say *no* to complain you say *yes* to gratitude.

Setbacks can turn us back to sit back, and count the Lord's unnumbered pay backs, especially to those who faithfully and gratefully serve Him.

Negative feedback and our set back must not turn us back to a life that is outback, but it should help us look back with a grateful heart.

Troubles could be God's way of getting our attention so He can use us, and make us more fulfilled and thankful.

The sacrifices of our war veterans for the sake of our country must be appreciated by this generation, and the generations to come. It earned them a lasting, and eternal gratitude for their sacrificial attitude in the midst of conflicts and war.

Be thankful or you may end up complaining in everything.

One of the best tools to resist the devil's temptation other than the Word of God, and the rebuke "by the blood of the Lamb" is our gratitude to God and the Lord Jesus Christ.

I'm grateful to God for the technologies: my mind, my thoughts, and what's in my heart can be transmitted or travel way faster than sound. God's answers to my prayers can do more than the former.

Words are not enough to say "Thank you" to God for what He has done in me and through me.

Courtesy and humility is spelled out in gratitude.

My gratitude to God who picked me up when I was down is priceless.

Express your gratitude to God for the little things that you have right now, and then you may ask or desire for more…

Be it an easy life or you may have been hit hard, and suffering from something that are beyond your control… but be sure to keep the high level of gratitude with your positive attitude.

My Prayer

I'm may be stressed out Lord, but I don't want to be out… I may have some pressures Lord, but I don't want to live and focus on pleasure… I may have some trials Lord… but I don't want to live in failures… And I know I can always pray, and express my gratitude to Thee no matter how difficult life could be… In Jesus name. Amen.

Our faith may have been tested, but we can trust God with a grateful heart.

Sufferings can cause unhappy life and a heavy heart, but thankfulness to God will balance the situations.

Material and financial abundance could not make us a happy family or make us feel blessed, but a thankful hearts will definitely be a family blessed by God.

Even if I have everything this life can offer, and everything are going fine and well, but if I'm unthankful to God, I'm in the opposite side of life.

Happiness is not a result of something we possess, but it's the recognition, and appreciation of something that we have and we don't have as well.

Five things that you can share, and leave to your love ones: love, respect, hope in God, time and gratitude.

A little of your gratitude can make an impact to a multitude.

In your prosperity- Praise God! In your poverty- Trust God! In your pain- Hold on to God! And in everything- Thank God!

When you pray, express your gratitude to God for people around you, because someone from the multitudes may have expressed their gratitude to God for you.

Every circumstance in life is an opportunity to be thankful to God, and appreciate everything even those that are beyond our control.

If the Lord gave us 24 hours a day, 60 seconds a minute; how many times did you say "Thank you" to Him in 10,080 minutes.

We praise and thank God and we express our gratitude to our love ones, friends who cares and loves us; but have you ever thank the Lord for those who tried to destroy you, criticize you, used you, made fun of you or persecuted you? (Matthew 5:9- 12)

Start your day with a thankful heart, and begin to thank the Lord with little things in life. Let the Lord close your day with the same attitude of gratitude for giving you a grateful spirit.

Count your blessings name them one by one, and then pause for a moment to count on those who have blessed you for making you to be a blessing to others. God must be on the first order, and must be on the center.

Life will be in a low altitude of gratitude without our burdens, our cares, people around us, and our gratefulness to God.

You may slip and stumble one day; but get up, stand up, and look up to God with appreciation in life, and in what He has done in you and for you.

Don't expect something great if you can't take a break and say; "Thank you Lord..."

A person who abides in His Word will always say the good words. I believe "thank you" is the magic words in spite of our negative circumstances.

Don't expect any gratitude or a grateful heart from anybody at anytime. Unfairness and forgetfulness are more popular.

I'm not blind, deaf or dumb that I can't express my gratitude, and make it as my attitude.

The difference between "gratitude" and "servitude" are the first 4 letters; therefore exercise both and you will make a difference in your attitude and aptitude.

The substance of our faith in God, and our response to His love must be express in 2 words- "Thank you".

Our worship to God, our love for His Word, and our commitment to the ministry are a good combination of our appreciation to Him as our King.

"Happiness and gratefulness" – Both are essential in every success.

Our heart is empty without God, and it is half full without our gratitude to Him.

The happiest soul is the sweetest soul, because he or she knows how to say "thank you" to God.

To love is to appreciate, and to hate could be an expression of ungratefulness.

It is impossible to live a life with humility, and not have the spirit of thankfulness.

A joyful life is a thankful life, and a grateful life is a happy life. And a fulfilled life is a grateful life.

Someone's life can be changed if someone would be grateful enough for the free gift of salvation that we received from God, and made a way to share it to others. It is an expression of gratitude to the One Who gave it to us.

If you lost the sense of gratitude, the next thing could be the right attitude.

We celebrate Thanksgiving Day once a year with festivity at home and everywhere. But heaven is a place filled with loving and thankful people. Thus, every day is *Thanksgiving Day* in heaven.

There is no valid reason why I should not be thankful even in a very desperate situation.

God's holiness and grace made me look up to Him with gratefulness.

I am always a student of attitude in gratitude of which I've always wanted to have a high aptitude in giving honor to God of whom I am very thankful about...

If I can't be the best I can in gratefulness, I may have a little problem of carelessness and restlessness.

My life is overflowing with abundance and joy because I learned to be thankful even with things that I don't have.

I may not have everything I wanted in this life, but I learn to be thankful for what I already have, then I can be content, and satisfied with God.

My desire is to help those who are in need; especially those who need to be grateful to God for all the goodness that He has bestowed upon us.

When you share your love to others, you also share your gratefulness to God for His love for you.

Giving God the honor, the praise, and the glory is not enough to express my gratitude to Him for what He has done in my life- thank you Lord.

You may be working as a wait staff or a laborer in a production plant nearby, but you must be thankful for the job, and being able to work for your family, for yourself or for the future of your children. Someone out there can't even lift up a pen or hold on onto a spoon or glass of water.

It's not about what you can afford to do, but it's about who made you do the things you need to do, and be thankful to Him who help you get up, work, walk, and play.

Gratitude is your wealth that destroys the ugliness of poverty and complaint. Money should not be the only reason to be thankful to God.

"Thank you" is the sweetest words a man can utter that could make our day.

The absence of peace and happiness should not make us cease to be grateful to God.

No matter what's going on in our life, let's make sure to start and end our day with gratitude to God.

Gratefulness and arrogance are words that don't match and don't go together. Ungrateful people are proud and high minded. Give and be thankful you're able to give!

Be thankful even if you don't have everything you wanted in this life. It means God is not done with you yet, and He may have opened the door for you to pray.

He set the seventh day to make it holy which would be another God's show of love and generosity to the sinful humanity.

We longed to be appreciated, and we complain because no one seemed to care. Now you know what the Lord felt every second of every minute, and every minute of every hour.

As you get up in the morning; you open your eyes, open your lips, open your mind, open your heart and say; "Thank you, Lord".

When was the Last Time You Say, "Thank You"?

Thanks to the Following:

My loving and dedicated wife Vemerlyn Dumala Sagansay
Reverend Eladio "Lad' Datuin
Eliezer Dumala Sagansay
Johnsley Lindongan
Arturo Raymundo Jr.
Joe and Ann Hurst
Mr. and Mrs. Benny Bernal
Wikipedia
Billy Graham
Squire Parsons
Holy Bible (KJV, NET, NIV)
Andy Sarmiento
Judy Tieng
Elmer John "EJ" Dumala Sagansay
Don Moen
Smith, Henry
Johnson Oatman Jr.

Ely Roque Sagansay

Edwin Excell
Faith, Prayer & Tract League, Grand Rapids, MI 49504
Cicero
www.great-inspirational-quotes.com
Charles Haddon Spurgeon

VISIT US AT:

www.ely-roque-sagansay.com
www.twitter.com/ElyRoqueSagansa
www.midailydevotion.blogspot.com
www.facebook.com/elyroquesagansay
www.facebook.com/MiDailyDevotion
Email: *esagansay@yahoo.com*
esagansay@gmail.com
Text: *(313) 850 0641*
Order your copy of Mi Daily Devotion
(Edition 1 & 2) and "Christmas Every Day"

Pastor Ely Roque Sagansay's Published Books

Order Your Copy Now

Ely Roque Sagansay

Reverend Ely Roque Sagansay was born in Bacolod City, Philippines. He grew up in a Christian home, and four (4) of his siblings are in the pastorate. He is a graduate of International Baptist Theological College of Mandaluyong, Metro Manila, Philippines. He's been a pastor for 3 decades. He came to know the Lord Jesus Christ April of 1982. Pastor Ely is a teacher, and a radio host of the program *"Gideon 300"* at DWGO AM Radio based in Olongapo City, Philippines. Pastor Ely started the radio program *"Love is the Reason"* aired on Light House Radio 106.3 FM. Ely was a professor, and administrator of International Baptist Theological College extension school in Subic, Zambales. He has served as director of music at the Greater Detroit Baptist Association of the Southern Baptist Convention (SBC). He pioneered International Community Christian Church in Trenton, Michigan- (SBC). Pastor Ely is the author of *Christmas Every Day* with Xulon Press and *Mi Daily Devotion (First and Second Edition)* with Westbow Press. He is the founder, and owner of the devotional site on the internet at www.facebook.com/midailydevotion and http://www.midailydevotion.blogspot.com

Pastor Ely is married to former Vemerlyn Dumala from the Southern part of the Philippines. They were blessed by the Lord with four (4) children; Eliezer, Ely JR, Eliel Lyn and

Elmer John (EJ). Ely's children are all serving the Lord in the music ministry of International Community Christian Church. His new published book *"Thanksgiving Every Day"* was born in his heart during tough times of his life, and family. Pastor Ely Roque Sagansay is very passionate about missions and he loves missionaries. He is a man of God and a man for God and for His glory.

Thanksgiving Every Day will help you look at life in a different way, take you into God's pathway, and will compel you to celebrate Thanksgiving Day in a right way.

This book will lead you to live a life with gratefulness, and a thankful heart in the midst of a complicated world that we live in. *Thanksgiving Every Day* will help you take a step of faith to the road of life filled with appreciation. You will absolutely thank the Lord you own this book. You will be surprise by the blessings of *Thanksgiving Every Day* Family Devotional. Be Thankful and Big Thanks!

Endorsement

What are you thankful for at this moment? Who are you giving your thanks to when you are in the act of thanksgiving? Thanksgiving is a huge part in our worship to God. When we are giving thanks, we are celebrating something that we value and we appreciate. Giving thanks to God is an act of worship that put us in a humble perspective. We are where we are, and we have what we have; because of God's generosity and love for us. Pastor Ely Roque Sagansay's new book *Thanksgiving Every Day* will encourage you to dig in deeper to the Word of God, and you will learn that thanksgiving is a big part in worship. It will benefit you, your church or ministry as what it did in me.

Eliezer Dumala Sagansay
Pastor- International Community Christian Church
4049 Longmeadow Drive, Trenton, Michigan 48183 USA

Associates Degree in Applied Science in Nursing
Henry Ford Community College- Dearborn, Michigan

Music Producer/Song Writer/Sound Engineer
Owner- Music Prescription LLC- Taylor, Michigan